Roadside With
THE RM

Jim Blake

Well over half of the 2,123 RMs built were used to replace trolleybuses, and the archetypal former trolleybus route, as well as the last to operate RMs, was the very busy inner-suburban 253. This route was local to me in Islington, and I had also worked as a conductor on it, and 'bunching' was common due to its high frequency. This is typified on Saturday, 14th November 1987, a week before the 253's conversion to Metrobus and Titan O.P.O., as RM800 (AG) escorts two others through Clapton Common. Numerically, this RM had been new to the route in July 1961. The ultra-orthodox Jewish people in the picture illustrate why the 253 is nicknamed 'The Yiddisher Flyer', and are probably heading for the Bobov synagogue in Rookwood Road, opposite the former Stamford Hill trolleybus depot which operated RMs on the 253 for more than twenty-six years.

Roadside With
THE RM

Published by Visions International Entertainment Limited

ISBN: 978-1-9998056-3-0

© 2017 Jim Blake and Visions International Entertainment Limited

The Author asserts the moral right to be identified as the author of this work

Visions International Entertainment Limited
PO Box 12562, Chelmsford , Essex, CM3 3YA
e-mail: deltic15@aol.com

For details of other bus and transport-related products, please visit the Visions web site:
http://www.visionsinternational.biz

CONTENTS

INTRODUCTION

It is hard to believe that seventy years have passed since design work began on London's famous Routemaster buses, and almost sixty since their mass production and entry into service.

Somewhat bizarrely, the Routemaster concept could have evolved into a new fleet of London trolleybuses if London Transport had not decided to cancel their replacement of the surviving trams after the war, mostly in south London, and used motor buses instead. As things turned out, those surviving trams were replaced by the same RT-types that ousted virtually all pre-war and wartime double-deckers in the immediate post-war years. During that time, design work on the Routemaster quietly progressed, with the first prototype, RM1, being unveiled to the public in the autumn of 1954, while the last few dozen RTs and RTLs were still being delivered.

It was at that time that the Routemaster was proclaimed as being the replacement for London's large trolleybus fleet, numbering around 1,700 vehicles, which London Transport had recently announced would be withdrawn.

Ironically, some of the Routemaster's design features, notably its semi-chassisless construction, were derived from those employed on some of the last standard London trolleybuses. Other features incorporated or improved upon new techniques developed during World War Two, and even when the first two prototypes had been delivered, these were subjected to rigorous road tests before the first one entered trial service in February 1956.

Four prototypes were built in all, one (originally numbered CRL4) being a Green Line coach, and the three buses, RM1, RM2 and RML3 were tried in test service alongside RT-types between then and November 1959. The Green Line coach remained in use, but the buses were demoted to driver training duties when the first mass-entry into service of 'production' RMs used to replace trolleybuses took place in the East End. The 'L' in RML3's designation showed that it had a Leyland engine (as did CRL4), and several hundred RMs with A.E.C. engines had been built before any more were provided with Leyland engines, as eventually a few hundred also were.

RM1 and RM2 had bodies built by London Transport's Chiswick Works, with Park Royal assistance, RML3 was bodied by Weymann and CRL4 by Eastern Coachworks. The latter two would remain unique, since all other Routemasters, including the later RML, RMC, RMF, RCL, RMA and FRM varieties, were bodied by Park Royal.

The first 'production' Routemaster, RM8, was displayed at the 1958 Commercial Motor Show, though full-scale production did not actually get into its stride until the spring of 1959. A number of new RMs entered trial service in June of that year, working alongside RT-types on various busy routes serving the City and West End, until in November enough new Routemasters had been delivered and commissioned to replace the Commercial Road trolleybus routes 567, 569 and 665 from Poplar and West Ham depots.

The reason why the first production RM was numbered RM8 and not RM5 is that three complete sets of RM engines and running units were delivered, fitted with rudimentary lorry bodies, and used as test-rigs to simulate buses with various numbers of passengers along various busy routes. This was to gain experience of maintaining them and draw attention to any possible mechanical snags. When these tests were completed, the sets of engines and running units, which were theoretically RMs 5, 6 and 7, were bodied and incorporated within the standard fleet. Only two of these test rigs were actually used, and eventually all three appeared numbered RM341, 398 and 459 - the numbers RM5, 6 and 7 were in fact entirely different vehicles, delivered as complete buses from Park Royal.

Even after their mass introduction into service, tests were carried out with such things as mechanical and electrical equipment, and suspension, which differed between batches of vehicles in order to evaluate which was the best. Little of this made any difference to the casual observer, though I can remember being made to feel physically sick riding on one of those with somewhat 'overactive' rear suspension when it was new on route 5 along the Commercial Road!

One quite striking visible difference between the early RMs and later examples was that the first 250 'production' vehicles had non-opening front upper deck windows. Ventilation was supposed to be made by the conductor opening a slat above them, with the same budget keys used to open blind-boxes, which let in air through an external 'lip' beneath the front dome. However, it seems few conductors did this, meaning the buses became stuffy upstairs in the summer, particularly as smoking was allowed on their upper decks. Therefore, subsequent RM-types all had quarter-drop opening windows fitted at the front.

Interestingly, a further one hundred bodies, originally fitted to RM255 - 354, had the ventilator slat above their front upper-deck windows, as well as opening windows. This implies that their body shells had been ordered to the original specification before the change was implemented. Interestingly, few RM bodies built originally with non-opening front upper deck windows were actually rebuilt with windows that did open, and until the refurbishments of the early 2000's involving examples re-acquired for use in London, this was only usually done if the vehicles sustained accident damage to their front domes and windows.

Routemasters were designed from the very outset to suit London Transport's overhaul system at Aldenham Works, whereby their bodies were separated from their 'chassis'. They have two sub-frames, A and B, which frequently became 'divorced' from one another, as well as from the bodies, at overhaul. Therefore, just as with the RTs, early bodies came out of overhaul bearing stock-numbers from much later vehicles, for instance there were several RMs with numbers in the 1800 and 1900s carrying bodies with non-opening front upper-deck windows. Similarly, many low-numbered RMs ended up with much later bodies.

Following the final replacement of London's trolleybuses in May 1962, production of standard RMs continued for another three years or so for the replacement of RT-types. At that time, the oldest RTs in use were fifteen years old, matching roughly their intended life expectancy. However, owing to Union disputes involving terms and conditions of their entry into service to replace RTs, it was not until December 1962 that the process began. By then, many Leyland-engined RMs had been delivered and were often allocated to routes where they replaced RTLs and RTWs, which had the same Leyland 0600 engines.

To 'muddy the waters', the first three trolleybus conversions in the spring and summer of 1959 did not use new Routemasters to replace them, but RTs and RTLs. This was partly because there was a huge surplus of these buses following massive service cuts in 1958, and partly because production of new RMs was running late. Thus only about the first 1,200 RMs actually replaced trolleybuses. By then, a trial batch of two dozen RMLs - literally 'Routemaster lengthened' - had been delivered, and most placed in service, and eventually 500 more of them were built between 1965 and 1968, as well as three types of Routemaster coach - the RMC and RCL for Green Line use and a batch of similar coaches, but with forward entrances, for use by British European Airways. These were acquired by London Transport after withdrawal by B.A, too, and along with the RMF and FRM types will be dealt with in separate volumes in this series.

The original life expectancy of RMs was about the same as that of the RTs, but by the time they began to reach that age, in the early 1970s, London Transport was beset by the twin perils of the shortage of spare parts and the disastrous performance of new, one-man-operated (O.M.O.) types such as the MB, SM and DMS which had been meant to replace them. Therefore, mass withdrawal of RMs did not begin until September 1982 (and even then as a result of one of the Thatcher regime's diktats and not L.T. policy), and it was not until December 2005 that the last were withdrawn from normal London service - a truly remarkable record!

Today, a tiny remnant of the once huge fleet of London Routemasters survives on route 15's heritage service between Tower Hill and Trafalgar Square. However, many more, now belonging to private concerns, may be seen in London in use for private hire and touring work. Indeed, the same is true for many other towns and cities in Britain, and also throughout the world. That in itself is a testament to their remarkable reliability and longevity: in fact, nowadays, in 'mainstream' parlance, ANY double-deck bus with a half-cab and rear open platform is referred to as a 'Routemaster'!

I was lucky to have been out and about with my camera in London during most of the Routemasters' long lives, and must have taken in excess of fifty thousand photographs of them. Therefore I am able to present just a few hundred of these in this, the first of three volumes showing London's Routemasters in their various roles and surroundings. This is by no means intended to be a full historical record of the RM class: that would require a much bigger volume than this and, besides, has been adequately done before! All of the photographs are my own, and many have not been published before.

My thanks go to the PSV Circle and London Omnibus Traction Society on whose records some of the historical details are based, also to my old friends Terry Handorff and John Gascoine who supplied me with the official London Transport overhaul programmes and variation sheets, between 1967 and 1986, which often kept me ahead of those groups' news-sheets! Thanks too go to Colin Clarke who painstakingly scanned all of my original negatives over some six years or so and to publisher Ken Carr for making this volume possible!

JIM BLAKE
Palmers Green
November 2017

PROTOTYPES

On a wet 18th January 1970, RM1 is flanked by two RTs in the yard of Barking Garage. By now it had been used as a driver trainer for more than ten years, and its frontal appearance altered to resemble a standard RM. This view provided an interesting comparison between the RM and the RT types; the latter were still being delivered when RM1 was first publicly displayed. And by coincidence, the last RTs in London Transport service were replaced by RMs at this same garage just over nine years later, in April 1979.

By 6th June 1982, both RM1 and RM2 had been adopted by the London Transport Museum, outside which they are on show along with various other historic vehicles. RM2, nearest the camera, had originally been in Country Area green livery and worked briefly on route 406. It later worked route 91 from Turnham Green Garage, for which it is blinded here, yet in the end, that route never gained an RM allocation. Ironically, the first mass withdrawals of RMs began three months after this picture was taken.

At lunchtime on 6th February 1967, RM3 heads along a remarkably deserted Waterloo Road apparently on training duties, although not displaying an 'L' plate. It is heading for nearby Cornwall Road bus stand, where those aboard will have their lunchbreak. Despite having non-standard Weymann bodywork, it has been rebuilt to resemble a standard RM and looks more like one than RM1 and RM2. It was originally numbered RML3, denoting that it had a Leyland engine. The 'L' was dropped when the first 30-foot long Routemasters, originally designated ER for 'extended Routemaster', were reclassified RML - 'Routemaster lengthened'.

Moving ahead to 3rd September 2004, RM3 is now RML3 again and has been restored to its original frontal appearance. It is now in the care of Cobham Bus Museum and is one of many guest vehicles running on route 73's last day of crew operation when turning right at Islington, Angel from the High Street into Pentonville Road as dusk falls. The 73 was one of the first routes to convert from RT-types to RM operation, in December 1962.

Although not strictly speaking a prototype, RM8 (SP) was the first production RM to be completed, and was unveiled to the public at the 1958 Commercial Motor Show. Curiously, though, it was then locked away in Chiswick Works as the 'Chiswick Experimental' bus, used for a variety of experiments for some seventeen years! Finally, it was overhauled in the spring of 1976, retaining its original body, and sent to Sidcup Garage, from which it works a 'short' of route 21 to Lewisham at Eltham Green on 17th April 1976 soon after entering service for the first time. It would only ever operate from that garage, being secured for preservation when the 21 converted to O.P.O. nine years later. It was then restored to original 1958 condition.

OVERHAULS AND BODY CHANGES

A brief word is necessary here to explain RMs' identities. Most Routemasters exchanged bodies upon overhaul at Aldenham, meaning in some cases an individual RM may have carried six different bodies during its London life; its original then five others on five succeeding overhauls.

Because RMs do not have an actual chassis, but a front and a rear sub-frame, these also became separated during overhaul, 'muddying the waters' even more. Therefore the 'RM62' which entered service in 1959 will usually be an entirely different 'RM62' from that which was running carrying that number many years later. This is why in the text which follows I often refer to an RM being numerically the same one that had,

for instance, worked a certain route many years before or after a given picture was taken.

All the two would really have in common was their stock- and registration numbers, although there were a few cases of RMs which, in theory, regained their original bodies on later overhauls, as did RM333 in 1981. However, although theoretically Routemasters' bodies always retained their original body numbers (for production vehicles, these were numbered B5-B2760 inclusive, matching the vehicles' stock-numbers), there is also evidence to suggest that, at least in the last years that Aldenham was overhauling them, some of these also exchanged identities - if only by error!

BUSES FOR TROLLEYBUSES

A group of Routemasters pass under the wires at Craven Park, on their way to Stonebridge Park trolleybus depot on 2nd January 1962, to replace the trolleys next day. The problem is they are not all NEW ones, but some have been transferred from West Ham garage where they had entered service two years previously! For some reason they were exchanged with new ones, and the two facing the camera, with RM177 leading, have non-opening front upper-deck windows. Stonebridge Park however also did receive brand new RMs, too, up to about the RM1060 mark.

RM809 (SF) is still in original condition, except for having is brake cooling grilles filled in, when passing Stoke Newington Station on 9th October 1965. It typifies the hundreds of RMs that replaced trolleybuses in north London in 1961 at Highgate, Edmonton, Wood Green, Stamford Hill and Finchley depots - literally knocking the heart out of the trolleybus network. It is based at Stamford Hill and will soon have its first overhaul. However, route 67 (which had replaced the 647 trolleybus in July 1961) will not keep RMs for very long - it converted to RML in December 1965, then to XA in the summer of 1966, reverted to RM in January 1970 but then converted to DMS O.M.O. in December 1971.

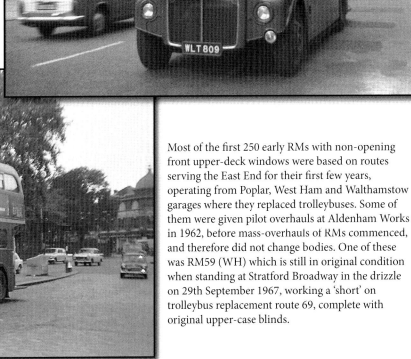

Most of the first 250 early RMs with non-opening front upper-deck windows were based on routes serving the East End for their first few years, operating from Poplar, West Ham and Walthamstow garages where they replaced trolleybuses. Some of them were given pilot overhauls at Aldenham Works in 1962, before mass-overhauls of RMs commenced, and therefore did not change bodies. One of these was RM59 (WH) which is still in original condition when standing at Stratford Broadway in the drizzle on 29th September 1967, working a 'short' on trolleybus replacement route 69, complete with original upper-case blinds.

Many trolleybus routes were replaced directly by new bus routes which followed exactly the same routeing. And example was route 269, which replaced the 629 trolleybus on 26th April 1961, running between Enfield Town and Tottenham Court Road, or 'Warren Street Station, Post Office Tower' as the blind on RM649 (WN) calls the terminus when approaching it on a snowy 10th December 1967. This RM had been new numerically to Wood Green Depot for this route, though by now had had its first overhaul. Route 269 was withdrawn amid the Reshaping Plan changes of 7th September 1968, replaced by an upgrade from RT to RM operation of route 29, which paralleled it all the way from this point to Wood Green, and a diversion of route 123 which covered it between Turnpike Lane Station and Enfield.

Dusk falls at Forest Gate on Sunday, 6th January 1968 as RM70 (WH) passes through on the 58's circuitous route from Walthamstow to Canning Town. Forest Gate Odeon, which was closed in 1975 and is now a mosque, may be seen lit up in the background. This RM too had retained its original body upon pilot overhaul in 1962, however it is not quite in original condition, in that its brake cooling grilles either side of the radiator have been filled in, unlike those on RM59 shown on the previous page. Next day, this RM went to Aldenham for its second overhaul, and the vehicle numbered RM70 which emerged as good as new had a much later body!

In pouring rain on 21st February 1968, RM152 (WW) typifies those that replaced trolleybuses at Walthamstow depot in 1960, but though apparently in original condition, has already had its first overhaul and bodychange, and will soon be due for a second. It has just changed crew in Forest Road, just south of 'The Bell' crossroads, and works route 275's rush hour extension to Enfield. This route was radically altered and converted to MB O.M.O. on 7th September 1968, with the section of route between here and Enfield replaced by a diversion of route 123.

A long-forgotten trolleybus replacement route is the 272, which replaced Stratford Circular routes 680 and 690 in February 1960, running around the loop in both directions. On 3rd May 1969, RM62 (WH) crosses the junction of Plashet Grove and Green Street in Forest Gate. The route was replaced by flat-fare route S1 using O.M.O. MBs in June 1969.

Once the trolleybuses based in the East End had been replaced, the last being withdrawn in April 1960, attentions were turned to north and west London. Hammersmith and Hanwell depots had their trolleybuses replaced in July and November 1960 respectively, whilst Highgate's route 611 which passed my home also fell to the Routemasters that July, then most of that depot's other trolleybus routes were replaced by RMs at the end of January 1961. RM400 (HT) and route 214 began service as a result, but by the time this view was taken, at Moorgate, Finsbury Square, on 11th May 1969, the RM had already had its first overhaul and body change. At first sight, it appears to be in original condition, but the lack of an offside route number blind and the adverts for the Victoria Line, give the game away that this is a later incarnation of RM400!

Many RMs which had replaced trolleybuses remained at their original garages for many years afterwards, at least numerically speaking. A good example is RM687 (EM), which had entered service at Edmonton Depot on 26th April 1961, and despite three overhauls and bodychanges (meaning that, really, only the stock number RM687 and registration WLT687 were involved!), remained there until the early 1980s. On 27th August 1972, it has recently had its second overhaul, and turns from Long Lane into Aldersgate Street on route 279's Sunday diversion to West Smithfield which covered route 4 between here and Islington, Angel. On the right may be seen the ruins of Aldersgate & Barbican Station, severely damaged in the 'second great fire of London' in the blitz of 29th December 1940, and the remains demolished at street level in 1955. The station was renamed Barbican in 1968, and new office blocks built above its entrance in the 1990s. Its platform-level structures remain virtually intact, apart from the overall roof destroyed in the blitz.

Trolleybus replacement routes 260 and 266, which paralleled each other between Hammersmith and Cricklewood retained RMs for well over twenty years. On 28th April 1984, RM1880 (W) calls at Willesden Green Station on a short working to Acton Vale. Numerically, this RM had only been in service for a couple of days when a tower crane collapsed on it in Leadenhall Street in the City when it had just replaced RTWs on route 15! Needless to say it was swiftly repaired.

Holloway, Nag's Head, was one of the busiest trolleybus junctions in London, and consequently when RM's replaced them there in 1960/61, also a focus of many different RM-operated routes. The last two trolleybus replacement routes operated by RMs served the area, too - the 279 which converted to O.P.O. in September 1987, and the 253 which did so two months later. On 10th August 1985, three RMs, RM562 (AG) and RM1306 (AG) on the 253 and RM200 (EM) on the 279, dominate the scene on the southern half of the Nag's Head one-way system, at the junction of Tollington Way and Holloway Road. The famous Jones Brothers department store on the right closed in 1990, some two years after the last RMs (on route 29) served this area.

ROUTEMASTERS FOR RTs

Brand new RM1311 (M) calls at Essex Road station, Canonbury on its first day of service replacing RTLs on route 73, 8th December 1962. Nearly two hundred new RMs had been stockpiled following the final trolleybus conversions in May 1962, originally intended to replace RTs on a 'garage by garage' basis with nine RMs replacing every ten RTs (since they seated more passengers). However, the busmens' unions objected to this, and eventually they entered service on a 'route by route, one for one' basis. The new buses that had been stored quickly entered service during December 1962 and January 1963, followed thereafter by further new deliveries. This one was Leyland-engined, as many were at this period.

Flanked by two other RMs, RM1748 (CF) is typical of those that replaced RTWs on route 24 in the autumn of 1963. It waits at the traffic lights at Parliament Square on 13th October 1965, a month before XAs took over the route for a six month trial period.

Route 14 was also typical of those that received RMs to replace RT-types (in the autumn of 1963) in that it was a busy cross-London route, but unusual in that it replaced RTWs from Putney, Chelverton Road garage, and RTs from Holloway. On 11th February 1967, one of the original allocation at the latter, RM1708 (J) passes Hornsey Road Baths on its way to Putney.

Route 30's RTLs were replaced by new RMs in the summer of 1964. One of these, RM1577 (AF) had a new feature - an illuminated offside advertisement panel, a feature perpetuated on many RMs and RMLs subsequently. A very wet 10th December 1967 finds it passing St. Pancras Town Hall when still in original condition, bound for Roehampton.

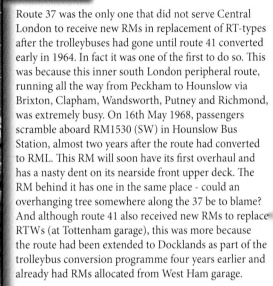

Route 37 was the only one that did not serve Central London to receive new RMs in replacement of RT-types after the trolleybuses had gone until route 41 converted early in 1964. In fact it was one of the first to do so. This was because this inner south London peripheral route, running all the way from Peckham to Hounslow via Brixton, Clapham, Wandsworth, Putney and Richmond, was extremely busy. On 16th May 1968, passengers scramble aboard RM1530 (SW) in Hounslow Bus Station, almost two years after the route had converted to RML. This RM will soon have its first overhaul and has a nasty dent on its nearside front upper deck. The RM behind it has one in the same place - could an overhanging tree somewhere along the 37 be to blame? And although route 41 also received new RMs to replace RTWs (at Tottenham garage), this was more because the route had been extended to Docklands as part of the trolleybus conversion programme four years earlier and already had RMs allocated from West Ham garage.

Many of the last RMs delivered replaced RTWs in early 1965 on routes such as the 6, 6A, 8, 8A and 46. Except for on the latter route, all however would be replaced by RMLs, but on 19th March 1968, RM2184 (AC) is substituting for one of the these on the 6 as it overtakes an RTL outside Charing Cross Station.

Route 140 should have converted from RT to RM operation in the summer of 1962, but the busmen's union refused to accept them, the main problem being that London Transport wanted nine RMs to replace ten RTs, thus reducing the number of buses allocated to the route and, for a start, lessening crews' opportunities for working overtime. Remarkably, it was to be a full sixteen years until the 140 finally received RMs in July 1978: was this merely for Schadenfreude; paying the crews back for thwarting LT's plans? On 3rd September 1978, a smart but far from new RM369 (which had, numerically at least, entered service eighteen years before) heads along Watling Avenue, Burnt Oak on a short working to Harrow. Less than five years later, in May 1983, RMs on route 140 were replaced by Metrobuses.

Until the very end of RT operation, RMs displaced from elsewhere were used to replace them. At lunchtime on the RTs' very last day, Saturday 7th April 1979, newly-overhauled RM1256 (BK) spews out a lot of exhaust fumes as it substitutes for RT1790 at Fair Cross, opposite Barking Garage. The RTs were run in and subbed by RMs at lunchtime in order that a farewell cavalcade of six of the RTs could be run in the afternoon. Ironically, RMs did not last long on route 62, being replaced by crew Titans early in 1980. Even more bizarre is that RM1256 was scrapped in 1990, but RT1790 survives today and has even seen service in London again when the Underground has been closed due to strike action!

DOCKLANDS

Route 40A began life, using RMs, in January 1965 as a replacement for route 48, which itself had replaced trolleybus route 569 five years earlier, running between North Woolwich and Aldgate, and on to Waterloo. Beyond Aldgate, it continued instead via existing route 40 to Herne Hill. RM1556 (Q), still with its original body, is heading there along the Commercial Road in Limehouse on 3rd April 1968. Just over ten years later, routes 40 and 40A were merged as the 40.

On a murky 30th November 1971, four days before route 67's conversion to DMS, RM860 (SF) crosses the swing-bridge in Wapping Lane over the London Docks' eastern section on its way to Wapping Station. The 67 had originally terminated at London Docks, and was extended to Wapping at the end of 1966.

RM127 (WH) accompanies RML2269 (T) at the Victoria & Albert Docks terminus on 27th May 1972. This had been built as a turning circle for the many trolleybuses that terminated here, but neither route 241 nor route 262 were trolleybus replacement routes. The 241 was introduced on 7th September 1968 to replace route 123 between Manor House and Tottenham, and route 41's extension from Tottenham Hale to the docks - both of which were trolleybus replacements. The 262 began life at the end of 1966, originally replacing route 249A on weekdays between the docks and Stratford, and the 26 from that point to Leyton (again both were trolleybus replacements), and was later extended to Chingford replacing the 249 also on 7th September 1968.

Right: On 4th October 1973, RM139 (WH) is one of two which have terminated at Holt Road, Silvertown, on route 58's rush hour extension there from Canning Town. RMs with such early bodies, immediately identified by non-opening front upper-deck windows, were still numerous in London's Docklands at this period, nearly fourteen years after they had first replaced trolleybuses in the area. The large building in the background is Tate & Lyle's sugar refinery; the little Victorian terrace houses behind the buses show that not all of these were destroyed in the blitz in this area, despite the terrible pounding they received.

Below: That same evening, RM192 (WH) and RM337 (Q) have the terminus at North Woolwich all to themselves. Route 69 had replaced trolleybus route 669 in February 1960, but route 40A had not been introduced until January 1965, replacing the North Woolwich to Aldgate section of route 48 which, in turn, had replaced trolleybus route 569 in November 1959.

On 1st June 1982, RM1244 (U) heads for North Woolwich as it crosses the swing-bridge at the entrance to King George V Dock on what had been a very busy Docklands route the 101. By now, however, the docks here were in terminal decline. The first RM withdrawals were on the horizon too, with the 101 losing them three months after this picture was taken, and this one was to suffer the ignominy of being used as a demonstration 'turnover bus' at a Chiswick Works open day a couple of years later!

On 13th October 1984, RM1527 (T) crosses Silvertown Viaduct on its way from North Woolwich to Chingford Mount, some three months before RM-types were finally replaced on route 69 by Titans. Nearly a quarter of a century after the demise of trolleybuses here, one of their traction standards is still in use as a lighting column and bus stop post, whilst two large ships may be seen in Royal Victoria Dock behind it: these too will soon be a memory in this area.

A new terminal stand has recently been provided at Canning Town, just off the Barking Road, on 2nd January 1985 as RM850 (WH) curtailed there on route 5 accompanies Titan T450 which had displaced RMs from route 58 a couple of years before at the same garage. The 5, which had already suffered almost ten years of the awful DMSs before reverting to RM/RML operation early in 1981, would follow suit in November.

IN SURBURBIA

Right: When new, most of the RMs either replaced trolleybuses, or RT-types that worked busy routes in central London. However, some routes they worked reached outer suburbia in the early days, too. Route 64 was the very first case of RMs replacing RTs, albeit indirectly since it was a supplementary allocation to its existing RTs from South Croydon Garage. A small handful went to Elmers End Garage when it was extended from West Croydon to Mitcham and Wimbledon Stadium to help with replacement of trolleybus route 630 in July 1960. This saw RMs running as far out as Addington, to where RM289 (TH) heads along Croham Road, Selsdon on 24th October 1971. The route had by then long been reallocated to Thornton Heath Garage and fully converted to RM operation but, however, converted to DMS O.M.O. six weeks after this picture was taken.

Centre: Another good example of RMs reaching London's outer suburbia was route 131, an existing RT-operated route that was extended from Kingston to Wimbledon to replace trolleybus route 604 in the final conversion stage of May 1962. On 6th October 1972, RM569 (AL) sets off from its Central Avenue, West Molesey terminus, actually well beyond the Greater London boundary, for Wimbledon. The route converted to DMS O.M.O. in May 1973.

Below: When RMs were replaced by RMLs on busy central London routes, and then later by O.M.O./O.P.O. types, they were often redeployed to replace RTs in outer London. The first route in outer south east London to received them was the 180, in the autumn of 1968. Some six years later, RM928 (TL) crosses the level crossing at Abbey Wood Station on 12th October 1974. Work is starting to replace the level crossing with a bridge, which will be seen later in this book.

Route 36B, which had gained RMs early in 1963, penetrated well into south east London suburbia. On 5th November 1974, RM1309 (PM) turns from Downham Way into Bromley Road at the start of its long journey to West Kilburn. The 36 group of routes converted to MD operation in the spring of 1976, but regained RMs four years later and would keep them until the end of January 2005, though by then, only the 36 remained and ventured no further south than Lewisham.

Routes 161, which had had RMs on Sundays since March 1975, and 161A converted fully to RM operation in May 1977, from Abbey Wood and Sidcup Garages, taking the type deep into south east London suburbia. On 25th August 1978, RM394 (AW) escorts another RM on route 180 in Powis Street, Woolwich as it sets off for Chislehurst. The 161A was merged with the 161 in September 1980, and in the following year its Abbey Wood allocation moved to the new Plumstead Garage and converted to crew MD at the end of October. Sidcup retained RMs on the route until it converted to Titan OPO in January 1985.

In the same area, the long and circuitous route 122, from Crystal Palace to Bexleyheath, converted from RT to RM operation in April 1978. On 14th September that year, RM51 (AM) crosses from Grand Depot Road into Woolwich New Road. RM operation on this route was quite short-lived, since it converted to crew MD operation early in 1980, swapping its RMs with them on the 36 group of routes.

Above: Route 105, running from Shepherd's Bush to Heathrow Airport, did not convert from RT to RM operation until the end of April 1978. Some of its journeys left the main route to serve Havelock Estate in Southall. On 2nd April 1979, RM353 (S) is one of two RMs at the terminus there. The route converted to Metrobus, initially still crew-operated, as a result of the 'Law Lords' cuts in September 1982.

Right: Route 83 was an early example of a route running entirely in suburbia that converted to RM operation and was not connected with trolleybus replacement. RMs displaced by new RMLs elsewhere replaced its RTs in the autumn of 1966. On 22nd September 1979, RM1090 (ON) passes through Brent Green on its circuitous route from Southall to Golders Green. This route too lost RMs in favour of Metrobuses amid the 'Law Lords' cuts of September 1982.

Local route 135 in northern Enfield did not convert from RT to RM operation until January 1978. On 24th June 1980, RM971 (E) is one of two heading south along Chase Side towards Enfield Town. The route was withdrawn three months later. The white-painted building on the right, at the time a dairy, was one of J.D. Wetherspoons' first pubs in north London when it opened in 1987, and is still going strong today.

Left: Route 193 had replaced the 693 trolleybus in August 1959, using RTs. At first extended all the way out to Upminster, it was cut back to Hornchurch in 1970 and was not converted to RM operation until October 1976, although they had worked it on Saturdays since the previous February. On 7th May 1981, RM1637 (AP) crosses the London, Tilbury & Southend and District Lines in Hacton Lane, on the route's recent extension there. The route converted to Titan OPO amid the 'Law Lords' cuts of September 1982.

Centre: On the same day as the previous picture, RM1744 (NS) climbs towards route 175's Hillrise Estate terminus in North Romford, to which it had been extended from Chase Cross in November 1979. This route had initially converted from RT to RMA operation in October 1975, and was not officially converted to RM operation until March 1977. Titans replaced them on a gradual basis in the summer of 1982.

Below: Although route 229 had been extended from Bexleyheath to Woolwich to replace trolleybus route 698 in March 1959, it also retained RT operation and did not convert to RMs until May 1977, when it was withdrawn west of Erith and rerouted at its southern end from Orpington Station to Farnborough. On 30th June 1982, RM311 (SP) turns from Bridgen Road into Elmwood Avenue, Bexley some two months before the route converted to OPO as a result of the 'Law Lords' cuts.

Above: Route 187 was a peculiar service that meandered through back streets most of its way from Hampstead Heath to Alperton Station, though it usually ran in two overlapping sections. It converted from RT to RM operation in February 1975, also losing them upon the 'Law Lords' cuts of September 1982. A couple of days before that happened, on 2nd September, RM941 (X) heads along All Souls Avenue, Harlesden on a short working to Park Royal Station.

Centre: A very peculiar development, unique in the RMs' history, was the establishment of Kingston Shoppers' Express routes K1 and K2 in November 1983. On 18th August 1984, an almost empty RM255 (NB) turns from Elgar Avenue into Ewell Road, Tolworth on the latter. Buses displayed yellow blinds. Just one bus worked each route, and they were reallocated to Norbiton Garage when Kingston closed in January 1984. The routes themselves were withdrawn a year later.

Below: The long 65, from Ealing to Chessington Zoo, also operated from Norbiton Garage, and ran through outer suburbia at its southern end. It had converted from RT to RM in October 1975, losing them in the summer of 1985. On 13th July that year, shortly before their replacement by Metrobuses, RM1273 (NB) passes through Copt Gilders Estate not far from its southern terminus.

PUBS AND ROUTEMASTERS

The Archway Tavern, more properly described as being in Upper Holloway than in 'Highgate' as bus blinds and maps erroneously described it for years, forms a backdrop to this view of RM1900 (R) setting off on route 27 for distant Teddington Station on Sunday, 3rd December 1967. The 27 did not convert daily to RM until June 1970, but fell to Metrobus O.P.O. in October 1986. Today, the pub is marooned in a pedestrianised 'island'. In this scene, works are just beginning to widen Archway Road, on the right.

Several traditional bus termini on pub forecourts survived well into the Routemaster era. One of the most famous was The Royal Forest Hotel on the edge of Epping Forest in Chingford. On 21st August 1968, RM258 (CT) accompanies RT4085 (T) and the London Transport canteen trailer that provided crews with refreshments at this terminus. Trolleybus replacement routes 249, 249A and 257 had been extended here from Chingford Mount, but were withdrawn on 7th September 1968 when the terminus itself was closed amid the first stage of the Reshaping Plan. Clapton Garage had only operated the 257 since the previous March. Each year on the anniversary of the terminus' closure, I am involved in re-creating this terminus with various preserved London buses.

Still bearing original upper-case blinds, RM763 (EM) passes The Goat in Ponders End High Street on 6th October 1971, shortly before the withdrawal of the weekday 279A, which ran from Tottenham Hale Station to Hammond Street. At the time of writing (September 2017), The Goat is the last traditional pub in Ponders End, and is under threat of closure. The wholesale closure of pubs in this area results from the increasing number of Muslims living there, whose religion forbids them to drink alcohol. Indeed, some pubs have actually been converted to mosques in north London!

The Hussar on Staines Road at Hounslow Heath was usually the terminus for journeys on route 117, once it had been converted to RM operation to replace trolleybus route 657, that ran to Shepherd's Bush. The 657's turning circle nearby was abandoned and RMs shared The Hussar stand with RTs on route 120. One of these is seen in the background, as RM1149 (AV) departs on 19th June 1973. The 117 usually ran in two overlapping sections at this period, the other being between Brentford and Egham, as it had run with RTs and as will be illustrated later.

The Green Dragon in Green Lanes, Winchmore Hill had been a bus terminus in the early days, and before the advent of J.D. Wetherspoons' pubs in this area thirty years or so ago had been my regular 'watering hole' for several years. Unfortunately, it was closed a couple of years ago and, apart from its facade, demolished to make way for housing and a Waitrose supermarket! On 26th February, 1977, RM1012 (WW) passes it on trolleybus replacement route 123, which had been altered on 7th September 1968 to run from Ilford to Enfield via Turnpike Lane. It was converted to DMS O.P.O. three weeks after this picture was taken, and withdrawn north of Winchmore Hill, where it terminated at Green Dragon Lane, just around the corner from the pub.

The George at Farnborough (Kent) was a traditional London bus terminus on the edge of the Central Area, where route 47 which came all the way from Stamford Hill and Shoreditch, and the 51 from Woolwich terminated, meeting effectively end-on. On 24th April 1977, RM786 (SP) occupies the stand, ready to return to Woolwich. Route 51 had converted from RT to RM in June 1976, but fell to DMS O.P.O. four weeks after this picture was taken.

Left: Displaying the destination 'Palmers Green, Cock', RM861 (AD) stands opposite the pub of that name, outside Palmers Green Garage on 27th December 1977 - my 30th birthday. Over the years, this destination display read 'Palmers Green Garage' previously, and 'Palmers Green, Green Lanes' subsequently. Unfortunately, the traditional Cock pub was later renamed 'The Manhattan' and after that 'The Faltering Fullback', before being closed and converted to a Polish supermarket in the early part of the present decade!

Centre: Recently overhauled RM2053 (U) sets off from Wanstead Station on route 101 for East Ham on 12th April 1978, ten days before the route's conversion to crew DM. On the right is the traditional pub, The George, which in more recent times has become a J.D. Wetherspoons' house. Behind the RM, the Terminus Cafe probably relates to the bus terminus around the corner in Woodbine Place, where at this period short workings on routes 10 and 20A terminated in addition to the frequent 101. Needless to say, the DMs' tenure on the 101 was not a happy one and it reverted to RM operation just eighteen months later, only to fall to T (Titan) operation as a result of the 'Law Lords' cuts of September 1982.

Below: The Fox and Hounds, some distance south of Chessington Zoo, was a convenient point at which to terminate odd school journeys on route 65 which were re-extended there along its old route towards Leatherhead in the late 1970s and early 1980s. RM2100 (NB) has just arrived there on Monday, 24th April 1978.

On 14th October 1978, football supporters heads for Spurs' ground as early-bodied RM760 (SF), complete with hand-painted registration plate, turns from Lansdowne Road into Tottenham High Road on a short working of route 97 to Dalston, Downham Road. This route had replaced the 67's northern section to Northumberland Park when that route converted to DMS in December 1971, but was withdrawn a fortnight after this picture was taken and replaced by an extension of route 76. The Red Lion pub on the right had a somewhat unsavoury reputation in the 1990s, and was badly damaged in the Tottenham riots in the summer of 2011. It is a shop today.

On 24th February 1979, just over a year after route 237's conversion from BL to RM operation and eastward extension to replace route 117's inner section, RM965 (AV) stands outside The Three Fishes pub in Sunbury Village, where the route now terminated. Along with The Flower Pot nearby, this had been a favourite 'watering hole' for me when pursuing RFs on the 237 a few years previously, and they would be visited again during the 1980s on trips there by RM. All a far cry from RM965's original haunts in my part of north London!

The crew of RM1757 (K) wait with their bus outside The Dysart Arms, Petersham on 9th August 1979, a time when routes 65 and 71 were severely disrupted by the infamous 'Petersham Hole', caused by road subsidence. Of note here are the two LT 'request' bus stop flags, one in red for buses the other in green for Green Line coaches, affixed directly to the pub sign. Sadly, this traditional Thames-side country pub is no more, although at least the buildings survive as residential accommodation.

For many years, The Favourite pub at Hornsey Rise was the northern terminus of route 14, on which RM425 (HT) departs from it on 18th March 1981 on a very short working to Kings Cross, leaving one of the scheduled RMLs - also working short to Green Park - on the stand. Although the pub survived the redevelopment works visible either side of it in this view, it has been demolished in more recent years, whilst route 14 was withdrawn north of Euston in February 1987 and replaced at this end by OPO route 14A which continued to Crouch End and Turnpike Lane. That has subsequently been renumbered as route 91.

Spring is near on 6th March 1982 as RM1744(NS) passes The Rabbits pub at Passingford Bridge, just south of the terminus to where route 175 had been re-extended shortly beforehand. The route had previously run even deeper into rural Essex, to Ongar, but with RTs, then for a couple of years journeys between there and Romford, localised as route 175A, were RM-operated in the mid-1970s. This pub made a good base from which to capture pictures of RM's on the 175's projection beyond Greater London, and served me well on several occasions in the early 1980's. RMs were replaced by Titans on the 175 a few months later, by which time it had been cut back again to North Romford.

For many years, The Manor House pub, at the junction of Seven Sisters Road and Green Lanes, was a local north London landmark, and gave its name to the Piccadilly Line tube station which opened adjacent to it in 1932. The original pub was in fact demolished as a result of construction of the tube, and the present building dates from 1930. Sadly, it is no longer a pub and now houses a shop and a cafe, with flats above. On 1st September 1982, RM1100 (AR) passes it on route 171, unusually turning short at Elephant & Castle. Just a few days later, this RM was one of the first to be withdrawn as a result of the 'Law Lords' service cuts. In common with most of these first victims, it had a Leyland engine and obsolete Sims electrical equipment.

On 20th November 1982, RM2143 (WW) stands at The Royal Oak, Canning Town terminus of route 58, shortly before its conversion to T (Titan) operation. The Country Area-style bus stop post with flag reading 'Authorised Bus Stand' is of note. Subsequently, a dedicated bus turning circle adjacent to the new housing development visible on the left replaced this stand, but today, a large bus station adjoining the railway station on the south side of the Barking Road suffices for buses terminating here.

By 10th August 1985, route 237 has replaced the 117's inner section to Shepherd's Bush, on which RM848 (V) stands in the company of a Metrobus on route 120 at The Hussar, Hounslow Heath. A plane above them heading in to land at Heathrow completes the scene. The 237 had been, most oddly, converted from BL O.P.O. to RM crew operation at the end of January 1978, and altered to run throughout from Sunbury Village to Shepherd's Bush. It converted to M O.P.O. in February 1987. RM848 is of interest on two counts. Firstly, it had received body B847 on overhaul in 1981 after that had been out of use for nearly eight years (on RM931). Secondly, after sale to Blackpool Corporation not long after this picture was taken, it eventually returned to London service in 2002 as will be shown later.

On a wet and miserable 11th November 1987, RM46 (AK) heads along Bayham Street, Camden Town, on the 137's long journey from Archway Station to Crystal Palace, ten days before the 137 was withdrawn north of Oxford Circus and replaced by new route 135 on that section. The Laurel Tree pub on the left was a favourite 'watering hole' both for bus crews on routes 3, 31, 53 and 74 which terminated nearby, and for train crews taking their breaks at Camden Town Northern Line station, until L.R.T. clamped down on such pursuits a year or two later with their 'drugs and alcohol' rules. The pub was also for several years the regular meeting place of the London Transport Gay Workers Group, which catered for British Rail staff as well. Alas, it is no longer the traditional Charrington's house it used to be!

The famous Spaniards Inn in Hampstead Lane was never served by RMs, but for several years in the 1990s they regularly passed it running 'dead' to and from Holloway Garage working route 139. In October 1996, RM1158 (HT) passes through the former tollgate at the up on its way to take up service at Golders Green. Camden Council's Public Transport Officer, Dominic West tried his utmost to get these journeys 'livened up', but London Regional Transport decreed them verboten since they would have detracted from revenue gained by route 210, which serves this stretch of road, and was at the time operated by Grey Green. At least today that route is double-decked, thus affording excellent view across Hampstead Heath to the City, which could have been enjoyed in the comfort of a Routemaster twenty years ago!

OVER AND UNDER BRIDGES

One of few cases where London RMs could cross above and below one another was Holborn Viaduct. On 19th December 1967, RM353 (HT) passes beneath it on the way to Honor Oak on route 63. Highgate had received a small allocation of RMs for this route in February 1961, when it was extended from Kings Cross to Parliament Hill Fields in connection with trolleybus replacement, which explains why this RM has upper-case via blinds. The major allocation on route 63, from Peckham garage, converted from RT to RM operation in the summer of 63. MDs would replace the RMs in the latter half of 1976, but RMs returned to the 63 between 1982 and 1985.

RM851 (SF) stands beneath the murky railway bridges at the site of the former London, Tilbury & Southend Railway's Leman Street station at route 67's old London Docks terminus on 30th November 1971, four days before the route converted to DMS. It was in this area that 'Jack The Ripper' committed his ghastly ritual murders some 83 years previously, and in 1971 even there were still some very elderly people alive around here that could remember his reign of terror!

Tower Bridge is one of London's most famous landmarks, but RMs only ever regularly traversed it at weekends, working route 78 between 1963 and 1972. On Sunday, 7th May 1972, RM1446 (PM) does so on the last day they were scheduled to do so, a week before the route converted to DMS. Odd ones substituted for RTs over the following five days, whilst, of course, RMs on sightseeing tours continue to cross Tower Bridge to this day.

Left: On a wet 8th July 1972, RM871 (FY) passes beneath the North London Line at Caledonian Road & Barnsbury station on route 263's extension from Archway to Kings Cross, which replaced route 17 at weekends. The 263 had been introduced in January 1971, replacing the 104 between Barnet Church and North Finchley and overlapping it as far as Archway. The route converted to DMS a week after this picture was taken. Somewhat perversely, the 263 still exists and today runs all the way from Barnet to Highbury Corner, covering the greater part of the old 104, which was finally withdrawn in August 1985.

Below: On 18th July 1972, just before route 106's ill-fated conversion to O.M.O. DMS, RM1098 (AR) passes beneath the Great Eastern main line in Grove Road, Mile End. It was at this location in June 1944 that the first German V1 'doodlebug' rocket to hit London fell. As for route 106, it was reconverted to RM at the end of March 1979, retaining them until the Law Lords cuts of September 1982 enforced its conversion to O.P.O. Titan working.

On 4th June 1973, RM216 (AD) passes beneath the Barking to Kentish Town line bridge at Harringay Stadium Station, on route 298's projection to Finsbury Park which was withdrawn just over a week later (though subsequently reintroduced between June 1975 and March 1977). Of note is the prominent advertisement on the bridge for greyhound racing at the stadium, once a very popular sports venue in the area. Now it is long gone, and the site occupied by retail units. However, the station, now referred to as Harringay Green Lanes, flourishes on the Gospel Oak to Barking Line of London Overground, being electrified as this book is compiled and due for extension at its eastern end. Route 298 still survives too, now running from Arnos Grove Station to Potters Bar. It converted to O.P.O. at the end of September 1980.

Right: On 12th May 1977, RM810 (SP) just fits beneath the railway bridge at Sidcup Station when working route 51A's rush hour extension to Charlton Station. This route, which had only been fully RM operated since the end of January, was withdrawn just over a week later. Until November 1958, when the road had been lowered beneath this bridge to accommodate double-deckers, buses passing here (on routes 228 and 241) had to be single-deck operated. The 51 was eventually extended north of Sidcup Station to replace the latter, and the 51A was a derivative of it.

Centre: On 21st April 1978, the last day of crew working on route 261 (Palmers Green Garage to Barnet, Chesterfield Road), RM798 (AD) passes beneath the impressive viaduct which carries the Piccadilly Line through Arnos Park and above Waterfall Road between Arnos Grove and Southgate Stations. Although route 261 had been RM-operated on Saturdays for some years, it was still officially RT-operated during the week until its conversion to DMS O.P.O. the day after this picture was taken. However, the last one had expired at Palmers Green at the end of March, so in practice, it was fully RM-operated during the week for some time before that. Today, route 184 covers most of the former route 261 in this area.

Below: For many years, the low railway bridge at Silver Street, Edmonton, under which the road is dipped to allow double-deckers through, caused problems in that in times of heavy rain, the dip was flooded, sometimes trapping buses and submerging them to at least waist level! All is clear, however on 20th June 1981, as an apparently empty RM859 (AD) heads for its home garage on route 102. The little girl on the right is my daughter Margaret, who was not quite four years old at the time. Route 102 converted to O.P.O. Metrobus as a result of the 'Law Lords' cuts in September 1982.

Three RMs are visible in this view of RM1960 (AG) passing beneath the bridge at Hackney Central station on its way to Clapham Common on route 35 on 26th August 1981. A banner on the bridge exhorts British Rail's new 'Crosstown Linkline', which had been introduced in May 1979, reinstating passenger services between Camden Road and Stratford - however, at first without any intermediate stations on the section east of Dalston which had been closed to passenger trains in 1944. Gradually, these were rebuilt and reopened: the old Hackney Station, just out of the picture on the left in this view, was replaced by the new Hackney Central, opened in May 1980. This is now an important interchange on the hugely successful London Overground system. In the meantime, route 35 converted to OPO in June 1986.

On 4th July 1985, RM1118 (T) crosses the Lea Valley Line at a dilapidated-looking Lea Bridge Station, shortly before it was closed. Happily, the station was rebuilt and reopened in May 2017 and now has a much better service than it did in 1985. As for route 55, this had been reverted to crew operation at the end of January 1981, having suffered just over eight years of very unhappy DMS OPO! The route was extended to parallel the 38 between Holborn and Victoria, but this RM has been curtailed at the 'Dilly, probably due to late running. By now, the 55 was mostly RML-operated, but it converted to Titan OPO in June 1987.

Nearing the end of its journey from Tottenham Court Road on 3rd May 1986, RM201 (MH) passes beneath Barnet Hill railway bridge shortly before route 134 converted to Metrobus OPO. This bridge was rebuilt in the early 1970s and carries the Northern Line of the Underground above the old Great North Road to their terminus at nearby High Barnet station. Tube trains were extended here in April 1940, replacing L.N.E.R. steam trains on the former G.N.R. branch. Alas, World War Two prevented the completion of the Northern Line's extension over the whole branch, with the section between Highgate and Finsbury Park, along with its subsidiary branch to Muswell Hill and Alexandra Palace, being abandoned after the war.

RM826 (AC) is covering for RMLs away for refurbishment by outside contractors when heading for its home on 11th July 1992, a week before this longstanding section of route 8 was replaced by the new 98 service. It is crossing the North London Line in Willesden Lane near Brondesbury Park Station, once a quiet place closed at weekends but now a busy station on the London Overground system.

London's last Routemasters in normal service crossed Westminster Bridge on route 159. On their final day, Saturday 9th December 2005, RM713 (BN) gleams in the weak winter sunshine as it heads for Marble Arch, on its last journey north. This RM had actually been re-imported from Italy as part of Transport for London's policy to return RMs to London service, and was one of the last to re-enter service less that three years before this picture was taken. It was refurbished at Arriva's Ponders End workshops adjacent to Enfield garage. On this final day, the last RMs and RMLs ran in around lunchtime, so that their final runs would be in daylight. In this view, the dozens of photographers on Westminster Bridge are not tourists, but those out to capture the last proper working Routemasters on film. My workplace in the years 1965-1973, County Hall, along with its then-abandoned and grotesque island block, form a backdrop to this picture.

HILLS AND ROUTEMASTERS

Above: Muswell Hill, on the Northern Heights, is one of the steepest in London. On 3rd May 1969, RM1964 (MH) sets off from route 212's terminus at the top of the hill for Finsbury Park. RMs worked this busy route at weekends, with RTs used during the week, until its withdrawal and replacement by flat-fare OMO MBS-worked route W7 a few days after this picture was taken. The traditional Green Man pub on the right has recently been converted to apartments, but a splendid new J.D. Wetherspoons house, The Mossy Well, opened on the other side of the hill a couple of years ago.

Centre: Autumn leaves fall around RM1886 (W) at the top of Shoot Up Hill as it heads for Neasden on 3rd November 1973. Route 16 had been one of the first to receive RMs in replacement of RTs, in December 1962. It was due for conversion to crew DMs six weeks later. The displaced RMs moved south to replace RTs on the 77 group of routes. The 16, and the associated 16A, lost their ill-fated DMs in May 1980, gaining RMLs many of which were ex-London Country, but converted to OPO Metrobus in November 1987.

Left: On 9th April 1976, RM1271 (WH) reaches the summit of Chingford Mount, closely followed by an early-bodied RM on route 69. This trolleybus replacement route had originally run only from North Woolwich to Stratford when introduced in February 1960, replacing the 669, but was extended to Chingford Mount the following April to replace the northern end of the 699 as well. In September 1968, it was further extended to Chingford Station, replacing route 249. In June 1973, it was cut back to Walthamstow Central and replaced by new route 269. However, it was reinstated through to Chingford in January 1976 and the 269 withdrawn, but then cut back again to Chingford Mount five years later. Titans replaced its RMs in the summer of 1984.

Right: On 12th March 1977, RM423 (SP) has just climbed steep Farnborough Hill on its way from Farnborough to Woolwich. RMs had replaced RTs on route 51 in June 1976, but were replaced themselves by DMSs in May 1977. RMs worked associated route 51A for an even shorter period of time, as related elsewhere in this volume.

Below: Nicely illustrating the topography of the Northern Heights, RM627 (AD) climbs Manor Road towards High Barnet on 18th April 1978, a few days before route 261 converted to DMS OPO. In theory, this route was still offficially RT-operated at the time, but by then, all of those at Palmers Green garage had gone, therefore extra RMs were allocated in the meantime.

Route 192 climbed a number of steep hills in the Woolwich area. On its last day of crew operation, 21st April 1978, RM1631 (NX) ascends Eglinton Hill, on its way to Shooters Hill and Lewisham. This route had only been operated by RMs daily since the end of April 1976, and this one typifies the scruffy condition for which New Cross garage was notorious at the time.

A steep, and as its name suggests, tortuous, hill in the outer suburbs of south London is Corkscrew Hill, in West Wickham. On 17th August 1978, RM1236 (TB) begins the ascent of this hill on its way from Bromley to West Croydon. Route 119 had converted from RT to RM operation in May 1976, and retained them until conversion to Titans in October 1984.

On 7th October 1978, RM109 (A) climbs steep Wimbledon Hill on its way from North Cheam to Putney Bridge Station. It was one of a number of early-bodied RMs that were having their third overhauls at this time; some of these would survive to have two more! Route 93 had had weekend working by RMs from Putney Garage since the mid-1960s, but was not fully converted to the type, by now operated mainly by Sutton Garage with a few Merton RMs on Saturdays, until the end of March 1976. They were replaced by Ds upon the Law Lords cuts of 4th September 1982.

RM2128 (SF) and RM1074 (HT) climb steep Aubert Park in Highbury on 25th November 1984, when buses between Holloway, Nag's Head and Finsbury Park Station were diverted owing to bridge works at the latter. Route 253, the famous 'Yiddisher Flyer', and routes 29, 279 and 279A with RMs (as well as O.P.O. services along Seven Sisters Road) were diverted via Holloway Road, Drayton Park and Aubert Park - the latter two roads normally being unserved by buses - then Highbury Park and Blackstock Road to follow routes 4 and 19 back to their normal line of route at Finsbury Park.

Richmond Hill is immortalised in an old English song, but Routemasters only served it for a few years, after route 71 was diverted over it late in 1980. On 13th July 1985, RM791 (K) passes through Richmond Hill shortly before the route converted to Metrobus.

On 28th October 1985, RM1822 (WN) climbs steep Crouch End Hill on busy route 41, shortly before its conversion to Metrobus OPO. The RMs had few problems climbing the steep hills here on the Northern Heights in snowy weather, whereas DMSs and Ms usually came grief!

One of many steep hills on London's Northern Heights takes route 19 from Finsbury Park to Highbury Barn. In March 1993, a few weeks before RMLs leased to Kentishbus took the route over, a re-registered RM346 (GM) crests the summit at Highbury Park. This RM was subsequently exported to Italy, but repatriated to London by Transport for London on Mayor Ken Livingstone's orders, refurbished by Arriva and returned to service on the same route in the spring of 2003! Displaced by the 19's O.P.O. conversion two years later, it ended up as one of London's very last RMs in normal service on route 159 in December 2005.

RMs IN THE RAIN

The umbrellas are out in Croydon High Street on 29th September 1967, as RM1325 (TC) sloshes through the rain on route 130 bound for Streatham Garage. It has just had its first overhaul, and before the year is out, this route will be upgraded to RML operation, using some of the last of that class to be delivered.

On a wet and dismal 28th October 1967, RM1239 (AF) approaches Kings Cross Station on its way from Hackney Wick to Roehampton on route 30. The bracket between decks towards its front offside is a 'BESI' bracket - housing equipment for bus electronic scanning indicators that were used in an attempt to replace roadside inspectors monitoring buses' progress on busy Central London routes. This RM had been stored for more than six months before entering service on route 37 from Putney, Chelverton Road Garage in December 1962. It is still in original condition here, apart from its nearside brake cooling grille filled in, and will have its first overhaul in December 1967. Route 30's conversion to O.P.O. (in February 1987) was unthinkable when this picture was taken!

Route 295 was a new service introduced in June 1967, running only between East Acton and Hammersmith Broadway, where RM371 (S) has terminated in pouring rain. The building on the right is the former Hammersmith trolleybus depot, now closed but latterly used by B.E.A. coaches, and the date 27th December 1967 - my 20th birthday. Route 295 was extended to Wandsworth on 7th September 1968, then converted to DMS O.M.O. in June 1972. It still exists today, linking Ladbroke Grove and Clapham Junction.

RM180 (WW) working trolleybus replacement route 257 heads for Chingford, Royal Forest Hotel as it escorts a Saunders-bodied RT on route 34 at Walthamstow, Crooked Billet in absolutely foul weather on 21st February 1968. Although appearing to be in original condition, the RM has already had its first overhaul and body-change, and will soon be due for its second. Route 257 was withdrawn amid the first stage of the Reshaping Plan on 7th September 1968.

Also in the East, the weather is equally wet and dismal on 18th January 1970, as RM72 (WH) changes crew on route 25 in Romford Road, Forest Gate. This point had been quite near to the old Forest Gate Garage in Green Street, but this closed in association with trolleybus replacement in the area, and its allocation for route 25 transferred to West Ham Garage. To reach this from here, crews had to travel on route 58. At this period, the 25 was only RM-operated at weekends. It converted to them daily in January 1972, losing them to Titan O.P.O. sixteen years later.

On 27th January 1972, RM1292 (Q) sloshes through the puddles on Albert Embankment on route 59A, which had been reduced to a Monday to Friday rush hours-only service at the end of October 1970. It also only ran to Charing Cross in the morning rush hour, terminating at Lambeth Bridge in the evenings. I was able to catch this picture simply because my office was on Albert Embankment at the time! The route was finally withdrawn five weeks after this picture was taken.

A very wet 30th October 1981 finds RM1851 (AW) running out of Abbey Wood Garage onto route 161. This was the last day of operation at this former tram depot when it, and the nearby ex-LGOC Plumstead Garage, were closed and replaced by the new Plumstead Garage. In addition, the allocation of route 161 was converted to crew MD operation, though its Sidcup allocation remained RM-operated until January 1985, when Titans, which had already replace the MDs in 1982/83, took over the whole route.

On 30th December 1986, RM232 (E) ploughs through heavy rain at Dalston Junction working the northern section of route 149. This ex-trolleybus route had lost its RMs to crew DMs in February 1974, but due to their appalling unreliability, they were replaced by former Green Line RCLs which had been retrieved from London Country and overhauled in the latter half of 1980. Four years later, RMs returned to the route, but it fell to O.P.O. Metrobuses six weeks after this picture was taken.

With headlights ablaze, RM2060 (CT) approaches Essex Road Station in torrential rain on 24th October 2005, just five days before route 38 converted to bendibus operation. It was the last Routemaster-operated service in north and east London. This RM was one of those bought back by Transport for London and refurbished, re-entering service in the summer of 2002 when route 38's frequency was increased, thereby needing more buses. As this book is compiled, it is one of the tiny renmant of London's Routemaster fleet still used on route 15's heritage service.

In an approximation of the 'General' livery it had carried for LT's Golden Jubilee in 1983, RM1933 (WH) arrives at Oxford Circus in pouring rain, unusually working route 15's 'heritage' service there to and from Paddington Basin. This was due to the Lord Mayor's Show in November 2009, which obstructed its usual route between the Tower of London and Trafalgar Square. Today, the 15's normal service ventures no further west than Regent Street. Of note is the bendibus behind the RM - these contraptions were now thankfully on the way out!

... AND THE ICE AND SNOW

On 9th December 1967, snow that had fallen the previous day is still evident as RM1296 (BN) passes its home garage, Brixton, on route 95. RMs had replaced the last RTWs on this route in May 1966, themselves being ousted by the first DMSs at the beginning of January 1971. In this view, it is remarkable how quiet busy Streatham Hill is on the third Saturday before Christmas!

Some snow and slush also still remains in West Croydon Bus Station on the same the day as RM1589 (TC) takes a break when awaiting departure for New Addington on the 130C Express. Subsequently replaced by the C-series routes initially operated by XA class Atlanteans, such a route is now rendered superfluous by Croydon Tramlink. Meanwhile, RM1589 was soon due for its first overhaul, and the 130 group of routes converted to RML at this period.

We actually had a white Christmas in 1970, and buses still ran on Christmas Day, too! Thus on 25th December that year, RM480 (HT) calls at the last stop in Upper Street, Islington on route 104's journey to Moorgate. At this time, the route was usually operated by Finchley RMLs, though this ended three weeks later and it was reallocated to Highgate (later renamed Holloway). Snow is still evident on the pavements here.

Right: Overnight snow on 30th/31st December 1978 has even carpeted Bishopsgate, along which RM1794 (AR) sets off from Liverpool Street Station on the Sunday 243A on New Year's Eve, 1978. Worse was to come in the new year of 1979, when roads were not gritted after heavy snow owing to a strike by local authority workers.

Centre: Heavy snowfall before and after Christmas 1981 caused havoc with bus services on the Northern Heights of London. After heavy snow early on 8th December 1981, RM2114 (AD) struggles through heavy traffic at Edmonton, Cambridge on route 102 in the morning rush hour. Sadly, this route which was (and still is) local to me converted to Metrobus O.P.O. nine months later. Of note is the 'Fares Fair' advert on the RM's nearside - it was this G.L.C. cheap fares policy that led to the route cuts that caused the 102's O.P.O. conversion, as explained elsewhere in these pages.

Bottom: On the same morning, RM1432 (AR) climbs up Tottenham Lane from Crouch End into Hornsey, heading for its home garage on the busy 41. Both photographs were taken on my way to 'work' at Hornsey Town Hall in Crouch End Broadway. On this occasion, RMs had no problems climbing the steep hills in this area, unlike DMSs and even new Metrobuses which could not manage them!

Left: On 11th December 1981, the snow is even heavier. At Turnpike Lane Station, RM1156 (AR) has been curtailed there on route 41, whilst RM647 (AR) is about to turn right into Green Lanes to battle its way home to Tottenham Garage.

Below: Around the corner, RM236 (AD) is also snowbound in Wood Green High Road, and it is a matter of opinion whether it will ever get to Mornington Crescent on route 29! At this period, the route usually worked in two overlapping sections during the week, Enfield to Mornington Crescent and Wood Green to Victoria, and was shared between Palmers Green, Wood Green and Holloway Garages. Latterly, there were also regular short workings between Turnpike Lane and Enfield, which effectively replaced OPO route W4. This service pattern lasted until it converted to O.P.O. in November 1988.

The snow is even worse on 21st December 1981, and has turned to black ice at the top of Tottenham Lane, so even the RMs cannot negotiate route 41 safely! RM1370 (AR) is one of three that have had to be abandoned at the roadside opposite Hornsey Police Station. On the left, a Mothers Pride bread van chances its luck.

Above: Snowfall on 6th January 1985 provides this wintry setting for RM1057 (SF) heading through Clapton Common on route 253, nicknamed 'the Yiddisher Flyer' by bus crews and passengers alike, since it linked the Jewish communities of the East End with those in Stamford Hill. When I was a conductor on this route in 1974/75, there were still many elderly people who travelled on it who spoke only Yiddish, never having learnt English despite settling in the area at the turn of the 19th and 20th centuries. The Yiddish language flourishes again today amongst the many ultra-orthodox Chassidim living in the Stamford Hill area, and route 253 ventures only as far east as Hackney Station now. A new route 254 overlaps it between Holloway and that point, continuing to Aldgate with both routes serving the 'core' section through Stamford Hill.

Centre: Very near to my home, then and still today, RM1822 (WN) on its way from Enfield to Victoria on the 29 has a nice wintry backdrop when approaching the junction of Green Lanes, Bourne Hill and Hedge Lane in Palmers Green on 6th February 1986 - thirty years to the day after RM1 first entered service, also in snowy conditions.

Bottom: This unusual view of a snowbound RM1590 (GM) which has turned short at Highbury Corner on route 19 on 6th February 1991 was taken from my office window in Upper Street. It also shows how the RM's special livery is quite a faithful replica of the General original, complete with grey roof.

SUNDAY SERVICES

For many years, several London bus services were different on Sundays, when traffic was lighter. Some routes were extended beyond their usual termini to replace others which ran only on weekdays, others had different type and garage allocations, whilst some only ran on Sundays themselves. One of the longest lasting, and longest, of the latter was route 59, which covered all of the weekday 59A, 109, 159 and 166 routes on Sundays - running all the way from West Hampstead to Chipstead Valley. On 26th November 1967, RM1591 (TC) pulls away from the stop outside Brixton Garage heading south. It still has its original body, and is derived from the 130 group of routes' allocation, which at this time was gradually converting to RML operation.

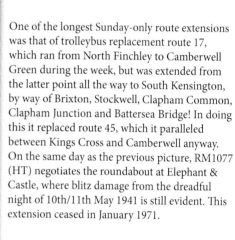

One of the longest Sunday-only route extensions was that of trolleybus replacement route 17, which ran from North Finchley to Camberwell Green during the week, but was extended from the latter point all the way to South Kensington, by way of Brixton, Stockwell, Clapham Common, Clapham Junction and Battersea Bridge! In doing this it replaced route 45, which it paralleled between Kings Cross and Camberwell anyway. On the same day as the previous picture, RM1077 (HT) negotiates the roundabout at Elephant & Castle, where blitz damage from the dreadful night of 10th/11th May 1941 is still evident. This extension ceased in January 1971.

A quite remarkable Sunday extension on which RMs operated was that of route 155 all the way to Hersham Station in Surrey! The buses worked from Norbiton Garage and were derived from the weekday allocation on route 131 which had originated when it converted to the type upon extension to Wimbledon in May 1962, replacing trolleybus route 604. The 155 was extended west of Wimbledon to replace the 131 as far as Walton-On-Thames. The further extension to Hersham, where journeys were only hourly, was added at the end of 1966, replacing route 264 beyond Walton-On-Thames, but was withdrawn on 7th September 1968. This view, also taken on 26th November 1967, sees recently-overhauled RM1338 (NB) passing Raynes Park Station. The 155 continued to replace the 131 on Sundays, latterly only as far as West Molesey, until May 1973 when the latter converted to DMS, but the route's main allocation from Merton Garage did not convert to RM until January 1977.

Some Sunday-only RM workings are now long forgotten. A good example is that of route 99, which was operated by Plumstead Garage during the week, but by Abbey Wood on Sundays. When route 180 from the latter garage converted to RM operation in October 1968, sufficient buses from it were available on Sundays to operate their small allocation on route 99. On 4th January 1970, three weeks before the route converted to MB O.M.O., RM1584 (AW) departs from Erith for Woolwich. This RM is of interest in that it is a product of body-changing upon overhaul at Aldenham, whereby RMs in its number range were having their first overhauls, and exchanging bodies with those carrying early bodies having their second one.

Sunday-only route 115A used RMs derived from Thornton Heath Garage's allocation of RMs for route 64. On 13th September 1970, RM1396 (TH) heads for Wallington at Mitcham, Cricketers. The route, along with the parent 115, converted to SMS O.M.O. at the beginning of January 1971.

On 19th September 1971, RM630 (TL) is one of two parked on the edge of Dartford Heath working Sunday-only route 124A's afternoon journeys to Bexley Mental Hospital. Converted from RT to RM operation in July 1971, this route then received O.M.O. DMSs in January 1972, making it, and the parent 124, two of the shortest-lived RM operations of all. A secure unit for mental patients incarcerated after committing serious crimes still exists at this location, though most of the site is now occupied by Bexley Park housing estate.

Left: Route 171A was a very long Sunday-only route that ran all the way from Tottenham to Abbey Wood, following the weekday 171 as far as New Cross, the 177 to Greenwich and then the 180. On 24th October 1971, with Bostall Woods as a backdrop, RM656 (NX) crosses Eynsham Drive bridge on its way into the Abbey Wood Estate. The route was replaced at this end by the Sunday-only 180A, also using RMs, in January 1972, and the 171 reintroduced on Sundays.

Centre: Route 9A was introduced in April 1971 as a Sunday-only service replacing route 9 between Mortlake and St. Paul's, then continuing via Great Tower Street and Tower Hill to Aldgate, in order to serve the Tower of London. On 7th May 1972, RM1967 (D) passes Trinity Square and the Port of London Authority headquarters, having set down its passengers for the Tower. The route was withdrawn at the end of October 1978 when the 9 was reintroduced on Sundays and routed this way to replace it, but reappeared briefly between February and April 1981. Today, route 15 follows its route between Aldgate and Aldwych, along with its 'heritage' service with the last remnants of London's RMs.

Below: What had once been referred to as a lunatic asylum, the former London County Council establishment at Banstead is now more politely referred to as Banstead Hospital on 29th July 1973 as RM1129 (S) arrives there on route 88's Sunday afternoon extension for the benefit of hospital visitors. Otherwise on Sundays, the route was extended to Belmont Station, but both extensions were withdrawn when route 280 was converted to DMS in January 1974. The 88 was unusual in that buses actually ran within the hospital grounds. The hospital was closed in 1986 and today, much of the land it occupied houses prisons as well as new housing developments.

Another far-flung extremity reached by RMs on Sundays was Caterham-On-The-Hill, to where they replaced RTs on route 197 on Sundays in the mid/late 1960s and early 1970s. On 18th August 1973, RM1208 (TC) terminates there. The route converted to DMS at the beginning of January 1974.

Another RM-operated Sunday working that reached the North Downs was the 59, which had been rerouted at its southern end to terminate at Old Coulsdon, Tudor Rose in October 1970. This is the location of this view of RM855 (AK), on a short working back to its home garage, on 9th February 1975; however, this is actually still within the London Borough of Croydon, whereas nearby Caterham is not. At this period, this famous Sunday-only route was operated by RMs from Streatham Garage and RMLs from South Croydon; the latter however were replaced by crew DMs upon the conversion of the 130 group of routes to that type three weeks after this picture was taken. These allocations remained until the 59 was withdrawn at the end of October 1978. Today, a daily route 59 serves the same roads as the original between Streatham Hill and Lambeth North Station, then continuing via Waterloo Bridge and Holborn to Kings Cross.

At the opposite end of the London Transport area, Sunday-only route 279A ran all the way from Hammond Street to Liverpool Street Station, though when this picture was taken on 13th May 1979, buses ran no further north than Waltham Cross. The route had been the first to convert from O.P.O. DMS to RM, the end of October 1978, and differed from the weekday 279 by running to Liverpool Street rather than Smithfield at its southern end. In this view, newly-overhauled RM1183 (E) stands outside the London Transport divisional offices at Manor House on a short working to Lower Edmonton Station (now renamed Edmonton Green) as RM1153 (EM) overtakes it on a through working from Liverpool Street to Waltham Cross. Extended to Hammond Street in September 1980, the route converted to O.P.O. Metrobus in late 1986 and was withdrawn in 1992.

Sunday-only route 243A had the distinction both of replacing the only longstanding suffixed trolleybus route, the 649A, and of being the last Sunday-only route operated by London Buses. It followed the weekday 243 (which replaced the 543 and 643 trolleybus routes) between Wood Green and Shoreditch, then originally continued to London Docks rather than Holborn. This leg of the route was altered to terminate at Liverpool Street Station in December 1971, upon the DMS conversion of route 67, which it had also replaced on Sundays. An oddity to work the route on 18th November 1979 was Shillibeer-liveried RM2160 (AR), caught passing Bruce Castle, Tottenham. This bus usually worked route 73 and was probably specially fielded on the 243A by enthusiast staff at its garage, since it was soon to be painted red again. At this time, the route was operated by RMs from Tottenham and RMLs from Stamford Hill Garage, but it later became all-RML, and was converted to Metrobus OPO in August 1985. It was withdrawn in 2000.

Roadside With THE RM

ALWAYS ON SATURDAY

Although Sunday-only RM-operated routes and allocations were quite commonplace in the 1960s and 1970s, those on Saturdays were much rarer. One of very few Saturday-only routes operated by RMs was the 245A, which replaced both the 226 and 245 on Saturdays, running between Stanmore and Cricklewood via the 245, then via the 226 to Golders Green. Things seem very quiet at its latter terminus where RM1439 (W) stands on 17th August 1968, three weeks before the route was withdrawn as part of the changes that took place on the first stage of LT's ill-fated Reshaping Plan.

Route 108A is always associated with Blackwall Tunnel, through which RMs never ran in service, but when the parent 108 was converted to MB O.M.O. in October 1968, the route was withdrawn through it, running only from Eltham to Greenwich, with Monday to Friday rush hour extensions to Surrey Docks Station. For a few months, it was RM-operated on Saturdays and Sundays, and on 26th May 1969, RM1248 (NX) stands at the Greenwich terminus. This route was withdrawn on 24th January 1970.

Pictures of RMs working north London route 244 (Winchmore Hill to Muswell Hill, with a rush hour extension to Archway Station) are not often seen, but they were scheduled on Saturdays from October 1969 until its conversion to SMS O.M.O. in January 1971. On 2nd May 1970, RM90 (MH) turns from Alexandra Park Road into Colney Hatch Lane. The 244 was withdrawn in 1982, but most of it is covered by route 299 today, except for the section between Southgate and Winchmore Hill, served instead by route 125.

Left: Another Saturday-only route operated by RMs was the 159A, which converted from RT to RM operation on 13th June 1970. RM877 (Q) crosses the West Coast Main Line in Abbey Road, Kilburn on its first day. The route covered the section of routeing between Marylebone and St. John's Wood used by weekday route 59A, instead of the 159, but was withdrawn at the end of October 1970, making it one of the shortest-lived RM operations of all.

Centre: An example of RM Saturday-only working was trolleybus replacement route 169, which began operation in August 1959 with RTs. Shared between Seven Kings and Barking Garages, it gained a weekend RM allocation from the latter when route 23 converted to the type in the spring of 1964. However, when the 23 was introduced on Sundays on 7th September 1968, workings reverted to RT that day and the 169 only operated RMs on Saturday. That situation ended when Barking lost its RM allocation on the 23 in July 1970. On the last day RMs worked the 169, 11th July 1970, RM1875 (BK) heads south along Horns Road, Newbury Park. The route would never gain a daily RM allocation, since it converted to DMS OMO in September 1973.

Below: Tram replacement route 181 was another destined never to have full RM-operation, having initially had them on Sundays between 1963 and 1966, then subsequently on Saturdays from the summer of 1967 until the end of 1970. On 5th December 1970, RM1578 (SW) may not have enough room for all the passengers waiting to board in Mitcham Lane four weeks before the dreadful SMSs took over this route! I wonder how they coped with such crowds? At any rate, the route was eventually discontinued in April 1981.

Route 141A began life in 1961, running throughout the former 179 route from Finsbury Park to Grove Park on Saturdays and Sundays only, a southern section of trolleybus replacement route 141 replacing the 179 during the week south of St. Paul's. After late 1969, the 141A only ran on Saturdays, still shared between Holloway (J) Garage RTs and New Cross RMs. On its northern section, between Ludgate Circus and Finsbury Park it replaced route 4A at weekends, and on its last day of operation, 28th August 1971, RM22 (NX) is on that section, at the junction of Highbury Grove and St. Paul's Road. A week later, a new route 4 was introduced replacing both the 4A and the 141A in conjunction with the closure of the old Holloway Garage.

Another route never destined to be fully worked by RMs was the 89, which gained a partial RM allocation from New Cross on Saturdays only in the spring of 1975. On 8th April 1978, RM703 (NX) passes the Blue Anchor pub in Bridgen a fortnight before the route converted to DMS O.P.O.

INTERCHANGE

Romford Station is an important interchange point between the Great Eastern main line and various local bus services. On 18th November 1967, RM1527 (NS), which has yet to have its first overhaul, calls there on route 174, which had received RMs displaced by RMLs on route 6 in July 1966, and would keep them until 1982. An RT on route 87 brings up the rear.

The winter sun casts long shadows at London Bridge Station on 4th December 1967, as an inspector gives the driver of RM189 (WW) his instructions, giving his 257 a short working to Hackney. This trolleybus replacement route was extended here from Liverpool Street when introduced in 1960, but replaced by new route 48 and a diversion of the 35 on 7th September 1968. Although appearing to be in original condition, the RM had been overhauled in 1963 prior to the abolition of offside route number blinds. London Bridge Station still shows the scars of wartime bombing, and the bus station here has been rebuilt three times since this picture was taken.

On a gloomy 14th January 1971, RM101 (PR) stands at the Finsbury Park Station, Station Place, terminus of route 106, an important interchange point between main line and suburban Great Northern services and the Piccadilly and Victoria Undergound lines, two bus stations and several trunk routes passing by in Seven Sisters Road. The structure behind the RM is the unfinished booking hall, facade and extra platforms for the Northern City line's extension from Drayton Park to Highgate and Alexandra Palace that should have opened in 1940, but was abandoned after the war. It was demolished in the latter part of 1972. A much larger bus station occupies this site today. Two days after this picture was taken, route 106 was withdrawn east of Blackwall Tunnel. The route then converted to DMS in July 1972, but reverted to RM again between March 1979 and September 1982.

One of the oddest interchanges on the London bus network is that at Newbury Park Station, where the peculiar-looking structure on the left was built in conjunction with the electrification of the former G.E.R./L.N.E.R. Hainault loop when it was taken over by the Central Line after the war. Used only for eastbound buses heading along Eastern Avenue, it might have seen more use if plans for a passenger airport at nearby Fairlop had come to fruition, but as it turned out, much of the land in that area remains open countryside - a far cry from the Victorian housing adjoining the abandoned Northern Line extension between Finsbury Park and Alexandra Palace! On 27th December 1971, my 24th birthday, RM1639 (NS) has called there on the Sunday 66B, and has few passengers aboard. A couple of weeks later, this route converted to SMS O.M.O.

On 13th June 1973, three days before route 241's conversion to DMS O.M.O., RM1778 (WH) passes Black Horse Road station on the Kentish Town – Barking line on its way to Manor House. This RM is one of many with high stocknumbers and early bodies that resulted from the intermingling of older and newer RMs upon overhaul at Aldenham. When the Victoria Line was built in the mid-1960s and provided with a station here (just out of the picture on the right), no provision was made for interchange with the adjacent British Railways line, probably because it was then slated for closure by the notorious Dr Beeching. However, subsequently the station seen here was demolished in 1981, and the platforms re-sited to the west of the bridge, with new direct access to the Underground station. Today, Blackhorse Road (as it is now spelt) provides an important interchange between the Victoria Line and the Barking to Gospel Oak London Overground service, which is being electrified as this book is compiled.

An unlikely interchange point between buses and British Rail trains served by red RMs was Egham Station, the western terminus of route 117. Well beyond the Greater London boundary, it was also served both by London Country RMLs and vehicles of fellow NBC subsidiary Aldervalley on 19th June 1973, when this picture of RM398 (AV) was taken there. Route 117 was cut back to Staines not long afterwards, and the RM is also of interest in that it was one of those overhauled in 1971 with a DMS-style 'unfilled' LT roundel behind its rearmost lower deck offside window, rather than a London Transport fleetname.

This view of RM1136 (Q) standing by the War Memorial outside Euston Station on 5th October 1973 unintentionally shows what the rebuilt station originally looked like before the addition of office, shops, a pub and bus station in front of it. Route 196 had been cut back to here from Tufnell Park when it converted from RT to RM in March 1971. It was diverted at Herne Hill to terminate at Brixton in January 1974, and lost RMs amid the 'Law Lords' cuts of September 1982.

A number of bus routes provide interchange with the Piccadilly Line at Oakwood Station. On 18th April 1978, RM615 (AD) has terminated there on route 298A, which provided a more interesting journey to Turnpike Lane than the Piccadilly Line. The 298A was effectively renumbered from the 29A amid the 7th September 1968 Reshaping Plan changes, using RTs. RMs replaced them in January 1970, but in September 1980, the route was replaced by a very long extension of route 121, when until then ran only between Chingford and Enfield. This still runs today, but its eastern terminus is now Enfield Lock, previously served by the 107A on which a new B20 DMS has also terminated at Oakwood in this picture. These awful vehicles were replaced by Metrobuses in the early 1980s and banished to south London; route 107A was later renumbered 307 and still runs today between Ponders End and Barnet.

Walthamstow Central Bus Station was opened adjacent to the existing ex-Great Eastern Railway Hoe Street Station in conjunction with the opening of the new Victoria Line tube in September 1968. It was also the focal point of route changes that took place as part of the first stage of the ill-fated Reshaping Plan a week later. Originally, it involved through buses doing a double-run off Hoe Street, which RM329 (WH) and RM690 (WH) are doing on 25th April 1981 on route 69. RM329 has recently had its fourth overhaul and carries one of the first hundred bodies (originally on RM255 - RM354) to have opening front upper-deck windows, and which also had the lip and opening slat above them, which is clearly visible here. The bus station has subsequently been rebuilt and enlarged twice, and is busier than ever at the time of writing.

When Turnpike Lane Station was opened on the Piccadilly Line's northern extension in 1932, a small compound adjacent to it was provided for buses terminating there. Trolleybuses on routes passing by in Green Lanes also had a turning circle there, then, also in conjunction with the Reshaping Plan's first stage in September 1968, a full-scale bus station was built there, with a number of flat-fare 'feeder' services replacing existing routes and connecting with the tube. By 12th October 1984, when RM75 (AD) departs from the bus station on a short journey to Enfield on route 29, these had replaced such trips on route 123 when the 29 was diverted there in March 1977, and by now had also replaced flat-fare O.P.O. route W4. The bus station here was almost doubled in size in the early part of the present century, still providing an important interchange between bus routes converging on Wood Green and the Piccadilly Line.

The forecourt of Victoria Station has long been used as a bus terminus, and on 13th September 1986, RM584 (AC) sets off for its home garage on route 52. This route converted to Metrobus O.P.O. six weeks later, almost exactly twenty years after it had first received RMs, which replaced RTLs.

On a murky 2nd March 1989, a battered RM1039 (X) calls at Westbourne Park Station on its way from Chelsea to Camden Town on route 31. The station shows signs both for the Underground's Hammersmith & City Line and British Rail services, but the latter stopped calling here not long afterwards, and the platforms these local trains called at were subsequently removed owing to track remodelling in the area. As for route 31, both this and the equally busy 28 which shared much of its route were converted direct from crew RM to midibus operation, much to the outrage of 'normal' passengers and enthusiasts alike, shortly after this picture was taken. Both routes thankfully reverted to double-deck operation in the early 2000's, but have been also revised in their routeing.

OUT IN THE STICKS

Prior to its withdrawal north of Barnet in April 1983, route 134 had a nice, fast stretch of route in open country between Hadley Highstone and Potters Bar. On 3rd October 1973, RM744 (PB) speeds along the old Great North Road on this section of route, heading for its home garage. The route converted to crew DMS a few weeks later, but regained RMs in September 1982. It retained them until O.P.O. conversion in May 1986, although it was withdrawn north of Barnet in April 1983, no longer serving the section seen here. Also of note in this picture is the London Transport Country Area-style request stop on the right.

One of the furthest points from Central London reached by red RMs was Chipping Ongar, to where they worked route 175A to and from Romford for a couple of years in the mid-1970s. On 26th July 1975, RM1451 (NS) heads along Ongar High Street near the end of its journey from Romford which took it well out of the Greater London area, serving the Essex villages of Stapleford Abbots, Passingford Bridge and Stanford Rivers. The route was withdrawn in January 1977 and replaced by a new route 247B with O.P.O. Titans.

One of the more bizarre red RM operations was that of route 146 on Sundays, which took them through open country to the village of Downe. On 24th April 1977, RM2021 (TB) heads through Keston Common, just under a year before the route, which was RT-operated during the week, converted to O.P.O. Despite this area's rural nature, however, it is entirely within the London Borough of Bromley.

An odd outpost of red RM operation was Noak Hill, Pentowan, where occasional journeys of route 174 were extended beyond its usual terminus at Tees Drive. Buses had to do a three-point turn into the entrance to a farm to turn around, and on 5th May 1978, RM1845 (NS) has just set off from there bound for Dagenham. The route had gained RMs in July 1966, losing them in September 1982. The Pentowan journeys, however, were withdrawn in May 1980.

Left: Routes 164 and 164A, operated by Sutton Garage, which converted from RT to RM operation in January 1977, penetrated well outside the Greater London area, to Epsom Station and Tattenham Corner respectively. On 23rd August 1978, RM434 (A) passes beneath the trees at Drift Bridge, near Epsom. This route converted to DMS O.P.O. at the end of March 1979; the 164A was withdrawn at the same time.

Below: In July 1981, route 175 was re-extended well beyond the Greater London boundary along its former route as far as Passingford Bridge. On 13th March 1982, low-bodied RM691 (NS) approaches the terminus with few passengers aboard. Over the next few months, the route gradually converted to crew Titan, and this extension was cut back again amid the cuts of 4th September. Today, a London bus route numbered 375 still reaches this outpost from Romford.

One of the longest projections of an RM-operated route outside Greater London was that of routes 279 and 279A to Hammond Street in Hertfordshire. These routes, originally introduced in April 1961 to replace trolleybus route 679, also replaced route 205 beyond Waltham Cross during the week, though it survived as a Sunday-only route (with RTs) until fifteen years later. On 16th May 1985, RM780 (E) climbs Dig Dag Hill towards Hammond Street terminus shortly before the 279 was cut back to Waltham Cross and replaced on this section by new route 359. It converted to Metrobus O.P.O. in September 1987. Today, no London buses venture beyond Waltham Cross.

THE ODD SPOT

An RM-operated route that is seldom seen, and often wrongly ignored in histories of London's buses, is the 137A. A relic of the 1951 Festival of Britain, it was a variation of route 137, running from Sloane Square to the Pleasure Gardens in Battersea Park that subsequently ran at Bank Holiday weekends. On Easter Monday, 7th April 1969, RM2060 (N) loads up in Sloane Street for the short journey to Battersea Park. The RM has yet to receive its first overhaul, but has had its brake cooling grilles filled in and lost its offside route number display. As this book is written, a later incarnation of RM2060 survives, just about, on route 15's 'heritage service'.

London bus drivers do not often get lost - well, they didn't when services were still operated by London Transport anyway - but on a snowy 15th February 1970, the driver of RM1120 (HT) on route 104 must have thought he was driving a 271 instead, as he has driven into Canonbury Road from Highbury Corner instead of Upper Street. He therefore corrects his mistake by turning right into select Georgian Canonbury Square, as illustrated here, and will continue into Canonbury Lane, from where he can turn left into Upper Street and the correct line of route. The latter is a very tight turn indeed! At this period, route 104 was operated daily by Finchley RMLs, with Highgate RMs added at weekends. The latter garage took the route over daily in January 1971, with RMLs displaced by DMSs on the 271, when it was withdrawn north of North Finchley. Converted to crew DM four years later, it regained RMs in the spring of 1981, only to convert to OPO amid the 'Law Lords' cuts of September 1982.

Left: On Derby Day, 6th June 1973, RM's worked a special service between Morden Station and Epsom Downs. At Tattenham Corner, an inspector guards an otherwise unattended RM2127 (AL) waiting to take up service. A special blue via blind has been provided for it.

Centre: Occasionally, RMs were given incorrect registration numbers, usually when repaired after accidents, but sometimes even upon repaint or overhaul at Aldenham. This has happened to RM1111 (T) which changes crew outside Leyton Garage on 15th April 1978. It should be 111CLT, not CLT111, and amusingly, RM111 (VLT111) was also on route 69 that day! In the background, demolition work is going on to buildings adjacent to Leyton Garage, to provide extra parking space for its buses. Leyton RMs and RMLs would work the 69 on Saturdays for some time after its main West Ham allocation converted to crew Titan, until it went O.P.O. in February 1985.

Below: New houses rise on the site of Canonbury Avenue, where I had lived between 1947 and 1973, as RM773 (EM) on the Sunday 279A escorts a DMS on route 271 along Canonbury Road on 13th May 1979, having been diverted along with other routes usually traversing Upper Street owing to Arsenal F.C.'s victory parade to Islington Town Hall after winning the F.A. cup the previous day. This route had converted from O.P.O. DMS to RM in October 1978.

On 28th July 1981, the day before the ill-fated marriage of Prince Charles and Lady Diana Spencer, a number of RMs operated a special tour of their wedding procession route through the City and West End. In addition to the special liveried RMs dressed up to celebrate the event which worked normal services for a few weeks before and after it, some ordinary RMs were also used to cope with the demand. Therefore a rather scruffy RM2044 (GM) heads west past Victoria Station in this view. Some of the monstrous modern office blocks behind it have now been demolished.

On the day of the wedding itself, 29th July 1981, extensive diversions to bus routes serving the City and West End took place to avoid the wedding procession route. Thus wedding-liveried RM219 (Q) finds itself passing Green Park Station on route 159, which was destined to be the last normal Routemaster-operated route more than 24 years later. The lack of other traffic along Piccadilly is strikingly evident.

On 24th August 1984, extra buses were laid on to work an additional service on route 69 between Stratford and Royal Victoria Dock in connection with the Powerboat Grand prix being held at the latter location. By this time, its main allocation from West Ham Garage had been converted to crew Titan operation, but RMs derived from route 25's were used, with special blind displays. RM1625 (WH) illustrates this when approaching Plaistow Station. The RM also carries posters supporting the Greater London Council, from which the Thatcher regime had snatched control of London Transport two months previously, and which they would destroy within the ensuing eighteen months. Also of note are the trolleybus traction standards still in use for street lighting nearly 25 years after the trolleybuses' demise here, and the line of black cabs awaiting trade at the station on the right.

On diversion on 27th August 1984, RM857 (CT) waits to turn right from Kingsland Road into Downham Road, Dalston owing to carriageway resurfacing on its normal route along Balls Pond Road; the RM following on the 38 is similarly diverted. They will then turn right again into Southgate Road where they will rejoin their correct route at Mildmay Park. Today, RM857 is smartly preserved in original 1961 livery. Meanwhile, route 30 converted to Titan O.P.O. in February 1987.

A very odd working on 29th August 1986 is that of RM167 (BW) working a free service to and from the new Asda store on the Ilse of Dogs, at which it arrives here. Redevelopment of this part of Docklands was just beginning at this period, and O.P.O. Titans usually worked this service. The RM has been customised for use on Bow's two crew-operated routes at the time, the 8 and the 25. After the latter's conversion to O.P.O. in January 1988, this RM ended up providing spares for others that had been sold to United Counties for use in Bedford and Corby.

Another case of a mis-registered RM is that of RM1810 (HT) which should be 810DYE, not 810CLT. It passes Mount Pleasant Post Office on the climb up Roesbery Avenue on 12th April 1988. Also of note is the upper-case via blind, as many London Northern buses were given at this period. Route 19 would end up with a mixed RM/RML allocation, converting to OPO in April 2005.

On 9th October 1988, a rock concert held in Docklands was provided with a special, free bus services from various locations in the East End. Most buses were Routemasters, and a contingent from Holloway Garage were meant to run to and from Central Park, Dagenham. However a union dispute blew up, meaning that most of these did not run, instead being parked outside Dagenham Civic Centre for most of the day! Re-registered early-bodied RM88 (HT) squeezes between a group of RMLs in this view. A rather rudimentary blind display is provided for the service, which however certainly is NOT running to Tufnell Park!

Atrocious weather dogged the Docklands event too, as shown in this view of RM613 (BW) running empty when crossing Silvertown Viaduct. Perhaps the fact it showed 'Private' blinds did not help; at least the Titan following has a notice in its windscreen showing what it is doing! This early-bodied RM has subsequently been smartly preserved, but also rebuilt with opening front upper-deck windows to resemble its original self.

OVERHAUL

Until its closure in the autumn of 1986, thanks to the Thatcher regime's destruction of London Transport, all Routemasters were overhauled at LT's huge Aldenham Works, most of them exchanging bodies and mechanical components at the same time, as the RT-types before them had. Before they were outshopped, they were given the famous tilt test, which ensured they could tip over as far as forty degrees without actually falling over. Visitors to the works were always shown this feature, as is the case with RM1264, which has just had its first overhaul on 9th November 1967, two months before older RMs having their second overhauls began to exchange bodies with those having their first.

An early example of a later-numbered RM being overhauled with a body from an early-numbered was that of RM1431 (PM). It has just been outshopped to Peckham Garage as it approaches Camberwell Green on 15th April 1968, the non-opening front upper deck windows immediately giving the game away that this is an early body, B160. Modifications at overhaul at this time involved extending the waistband right across the front, making the air intake grille beneath the blind-boxes narrower; filling in the brake-cooling grilles either side of the radiator grille; and altering the radiator grille to include the 'blue triangle' London Transport badge.

RM1633 looks as good as new when passing Oval Station on its way from its first overhaul at Aldenham to Peckham Garage on 20th March 1969. It is of note that at this period, newly-overhauled and repainted buses were given external advertisements at Aldenham before being sent to their respective garages.

In the summer of 1972, the last RMs had their first overhauls, after which the first production RMLs (from RML2261 onwards) went in for theirs. Because both classes were done on the 'Works Float' system, whereby buses changed bodies upon overhaul but because bodies took longer to overhaul than the mechanical components, a 'float' was needed, certain buses 'disappeared' onto the Works Float when overhauling of their types began. This had happened with the RMs, when full overhauls began in the summer of 1963 and certain early RMs, numbered between 5 and 33, became floats. This did not, of course, mean that the actual buses were simply stored at Aldenham and robbed of parts - the number of 'float' stocknumbers corresponded with the number of complete sets of 'discarnate' body and mechanical parts for the relevant class which were in works for overhaul at any given time. So when the number of RMs being overhauled was reduced to make way for RMLs (a number of which also became Works Floats), certain of the RM stocknumbers which had not been seen since the early part of 1963 reappeared. On 12th July 1972, one of these, RM5, awaits return to service at Aldenham Works. It has body B2203, which in common with other early RM stocknumbers released from float at that time, came from one of the last few RMs to be delivered in the spring of 1965 then having their first overhauls.

At Aldenham Works on 4th October 1972, the body hitherto carried by RM737 (B782), has been divorced from its 'chassis' sub-frames and is being rotated on one of the works' famous inverters, in order to give its undercarriage a through steam-cleaning to remove some seven years' worth of grease and dirt by this time, the time between RMs' overhauls had been lengthened to approximately seven years. Unlike the RTs' bodies which suffered from wood rot and rust, those on RMs did not, being primarily constructed in aluminium and fibreglass. This body emerged as RM707.

On the same day, at the other end of the works, Routemasters predominate after passing through the paint-shop, before being finally checked out in the licensing shop. However, RM1678, the only one identifiable in this picture has only had an inter-overhaul repaint, not a full overhaul. Nevertheless, the standard of external painting at this period was still first class even for buses having these. The Routemaster nearest the camera in this view is in fact an RML, overhauls for the first production examples of these having begun at Aldenham in the summer of 1972.

On 16th May 1977, RM681 also looks as good as new when caught speeding past New Barnet Station on its way from its third overhaul at Aldenham to Edmonton Garage, which was its original home (numerically, anyway!) more than sixteen years earlier.

Ten days after the previous picture was taken, at Aldenham Works itself, on 26th May 1977, an early RM body, body B210 ex-RM42, by now almost eighteen years old, is given the full works on one of the inverters during overhaul. It emerged as RM128 in July. Had the MB, SM and DM types not been such a disaster, RMs with bodies of this age would by now be due for withdrawal, but no one in 1977 could have foreseen that some would last until the very end in 2005!

On the same occasion, three RMs stand outside Aldenham Works after overhaul awaiting their turn in the paint shop. This view nicely illustrates how, during the process, they were extensively repanelled in instances where their panels had been dented. Some panels were new, others were used ones which had been repaired, and the ribbing between them perfectly matches the analogy of a Routemaster bus to a Meccano set! Nearest the camera is body B108, recently shed by RM205 whose number is still shown on the cabside. It emerged as RM745 in July, meanwhile the number 'RM205' disappeared onto Works Float at this time, but reappeared in June 1978: such were the eccentricities of the Aldenham overhaul system!

Painting completed, early-bodied RM691 and RM45 await their turn in the licensing shop, and accompany a staff bus RT and a defunct DMS outside the works. Of these two, RM45 would subsequently have a remarkable history, as related elsewhere in this volume.

t Aldenham Works, bodies removed from the buses' chassis and running units were lifted high above others awaiting attention on a travelling crane facilitate movement to different parts of the works during the overhaul process. On 18th September 1980, body B717, which had been on RM315, lustrates this. As is well-known, Aldenham was originally built as a depot and maintenance facility for the Northern Line of the Underground's tension from Edgware to Bushey Heath, on which work was unfortunately interrupted by the war and then abandoned after it. The works was dapted to build bomber aircraft during the war, and then for bus overhauling in the 1950s. Its external appearance was very similar to the new nderground depots built at Hainault and Ruislip, also as part of the 1935-1940 New Works Programme.

Things are not as they seem in this view of a Routemaster at Aldenham Works, apparently in mid-overhaul, also on 18th September 1980. Its running units have been overhauled, and part of its lower deck repanelled. However, its front dome is badly dented and has yet to be done. Most odd of all, is that also this is clearly a 64-seat, four-bay RM, yet its cabside number shows RML2543! Even more bizarrely, the RML of that number had been overhauled in July and been back in service for more than two months when this picture was taken!!

Newly-overhauled RM247 and two others await delivery from Aldenham Works to various garages on 25th March 1982, and still look as good as new. However at this period, buses were often sent out to garages without external advertising, which had to be applied after they had arrived there. This meant that they now often ran in service in this condition for a few days.

ALL-OVER ADVERTISMENTS

London buses have carried external advertising for many years, but in the summer of 1969, a new departure on this theme was the painting of RM1737 (R) in an all-over advertisement livery for Silexene Paints. The result approaches Trafalgar Square on the famous 11 route on 1st September that year. Long afterwards, the same RM, numerically, was adopted as a showbus at Ash Grove Garage and could again be seen on the 11, and of course today, many modern London buses carry all-over advertisements.

Left: The second such London bus, RM971 (D) also worked route 11. For Yellow Pages' Directories it bore a striking yellow and black livery. This view of it on 21st May 1971 finds it passing Victoria Station bound for Hammersmith, also on route 11. It later moved to route 88.

Below: All-over advertisements really took off during 1972, and one of the most bizarre was RM1270 which had a virtually psychedelic livery promoting Sharp Radios. On 21st May 1972, it has just been so adorned when taken on a private hire to promote the firm at the Bloomsbury Centre. It has also been misregistered CLT270 instead of 270CLT upon repaint. It later worked routes 22 and 73 until the end of 1973.

Also active on route 22, RM2140 (B) was in a basically purple livery advertising Bertorelli Ice Creams. It has just been done when caught passing Green Park Station on 23rd July 1972. Later used on routes 2B, 26, 88 and 159, it carried this livery until late 1973, too.

In a basically light blue livery advertising Vernons' football pools, RM686 (WN) calls at the long-lost Jones Brothers' department store on the Holloway, Nag's Head one-way system on 19th August 1972. By now such buses were becoming all the rage, and a number of RMLs also carried all-over advertisements. This one lasted well into 1974, later working such diverse routes as the 88, 53, 171, 38 and 18.

a basically light blue
very, RM762 (SF)
dvertised Esso Blue
araffin oil. Late autumn
unshine catches it
assing Lambeth Palace
n route 149's southern
xtension to Victoria on
0th November 1972. It
ter worked on routes
9, 2 and 8.

erhaps appropriately during the winter
f 1972/73, RM783 (SF) advertised Uniflo
nti-freeze but surely, London Transport were
utting their own throats advertising aids
or motorists? It is about to cross Lambeth
Bridge when crossing Millbank on a unusual
hort working of route 149 from Victoria to
Dalston, Downham Road on 23rd January
973. Later in 1973, it worked routes 2, 9/9A
nd 53 until the winter of that year.

Active during the spring
and summer of 1973
dvertising Ladbrokes, the
urf accountants, was RM786
which worked routes 13, 8
and 19. However on Derby
Day, 6th June 1973, it quite
appropriately promoted the
irm on Epsom Downs. An
RML also had an all-over
advertisment for this company.

Quite short-lived was the use of RM294 (GM) in a silver livery, not unlike that of the famous RM664 and the later SRMs, promoting Celebrity Travel on route 137. It negotiates the one-way system at Great Portland Street Station on 8th June 1973, heading for Archway Station.

RM682 (AE) in a basic white livery advertised Pye electrical equipment, and was based at Hendon Garage between May and November 1973. It worked route 13 during the week, but since that did not run on Sundays, it had to work the 113 that day. This explains its presence at Edgware Station on 24th June 1973. Curiously, all the passengers there seem to be boarding the SMS on route 142, rather than the RM.

Another short-lived advert appeared on RM1740 (AR) which was green and white livery advertising Donane Yoghurts on route 73. On 3rd July 1973, it crosses the junction of Upper Street, Liverpool Road and Islington High Street on its way from Stoke Newington to Hammersmith.

And another short-lived all-over advertisement RM was on RM995 (WN) which worked for a few months in the early part of 1974 on route 29, on which it heads south along Charing Cross Road on 25th March 1974. Livery was basically pink and white, advertising the Bank of Cyprus.

Perhaps the shortest-lived all-over advertisement at this period of all was that on RM1359 (SW) promoting the port of Boulogne. With a basic yellow livery, it loads up on route 88 in Parliament Street on 13th May 1974.

During 1973/74, RM1285 advertised Peter Dominic wine shops, and was mainly used on routes 9, 9A, 13 and 113. However on 4th June 1974 it is working route 102 from Palmers Green Garage, which it approaches on its way to Chingford in this view. Livery was basically dark blue and orange.

Between the summer of 1974 and spring of 1975, RM1255 (BW) worked route 8 in a mixture of yellow and purple livery promoting Rand 'temp' agencies. On 19th February 1975, it sets off from Willesden Garage for Old Ford, shortly before route 8 began to convert to RML operation.

Left: The last of the 1970s all-over advertisement RMs was RM1676 (NX) which, adorned in a pleasant green and grey/white livery, promoted English apples and pears. It worked routes 159 and 171 during the winter of 1975/76. It works the latter at Chancery Lane Station in the morning rush hour of 3rd February 1976.

Bottom: An afterthought in the 'all-over advertisement RM saga' was the appearance of RM1237 (B) in January 1980 advertising Wisdom toothbrushes. However the livery was basically red, so not as striking as the earlier vehicles, though as this view at route 22's Putney Common, Spencer Arms terminus shows, it lacked a waistband. It subsequently worked routes 29, 25 and 159 during the rest of the year. Three RMLs subsequently carried all-over adverts, however, in the mid-1980s.

MATCHING NUMBERS

Not only did most RMs have registration numbers that matched all or part of their stocknumbers, occasionally these matched their route numbers as well! A case in question is RM230 (T) which works new route 230 on its first day of operation, 16th June 1973. It leaves the new Stratford Bus Station, also opened that day. With a multi-storey car park above it, this place soon became a muggers' paradise, as well as an unofficial urinal thanks to its dark nooks an crannies. A larger and more pleasant bus station occupies the site today. Route 230 somewhat oddly converted from RM to single-deck LS O.P.O. at the end of January 1981.

Christmas shoppers abound in Wood Green High Road as RM1029 (HT) nears the end of its journey from Victoria on 6th December 1975, a week before this busy route's disastrous conversion to crew DM operation. This picture shows a number of things of interest other than the RM, for instance the three-wheeler car overtaking it and the High Road's late-lamented British Home Stores on the left. Route 29 would regain RMs in March 1977, keeping them until November 1988.

A remarkable appearance on 16th August 1977 is that of newly-overhauled RM217 (E) on route 217. This route had never been scheduled for RM operation, but at this period they did occasionally substitute for its usual RTs, which were replaced by O.P.O. DMSs four days after this picture was taken in Sun Street, Waltham Abbey. It was only in April 1976 that RMs at Ponders End Garage gained blinds for their RT-operated routes, when the new 217B was introduced using the latter.

Right: Sandwiched between two other Routemasters, RM137 (GM) calls at Selfridges in Oxford Street and, numerically, is a far cry from the RMs in the 2000 series which had replaced RTs and RTLs on route 137 in the autumn of 1964. The route would be Routemaster-operated for almost forty years, converting to O.P.O. in July 2004.

Below: On 18th August 1980, RM1076 (AR) crosses Stamford Hill Broadway in heavy traffic with its registration digits matching its route number. It was unusual for buses on route 76 to terminate at County Hall, presumably this is a curtailment due to late running. The route had officially converted to full RM operation in January 1970, succumbing to O.P.O. Metrobuses fifteen years later. It had used some of the first production RMLs which were used for comparative trials with the XAs in 1965/66, the latter remaining until replaced by RMs in 1970.

Below: A pocket of winter sunshine lights up RM12 (WL) working route 12 as it waits to turn right from the Uxbridge Road into Old Oak Road on this route's tortuously long journey from Norwood Junction to Willesden Junction on 27th December 1980 - my 33rd birthday. Usually, the route worked in overlapping sections, although some buses did run throughout. It was worked by four different garages at this period - Shepherd's Bush, Walworth, Peckham and Elmers End. It had had a very protracted conversion to RM between January and May 1973, and had a mixed allocation of RMs and RMLs when bendibuses replaced them in November 2004.

Right Routes 176 and 176A were the last RT-operated routes serving the West End and City respectively, which converted to RM operation in the spring of 1976. On 7th July 1981, RM2176 (WL) has unusually terminated at Charing Cross from the south, and runs around the block at Trafalgar Square to return. It wrongly shows a via blind for the 176A, which ran from Forest Hill to Cannon Street, parting company with the 176 at Elephant & Castle and crossing Southwark rather than Waterloo Bridge. The 176A was withdrawn amid the 'Law Lords' cuts of September 1982, but the 176 retained RMs until converted to Titans in the summer of 1984.

Below: RM47 (TB) stands in Lewisham Bus Station on 13th October 1981, working one of route 47's short journeys between that point and Farnborough. At the time, this RM carried body B5, numerically the first standard RM body, which it had gained on its last Aldenham overhaul. It was subsequently adopted as a showbus at Norwood Garage. Crew-operated Titans replaced RMs on route 47 in the summer of 1984, but RMs still appeared until it went OPO two years later.

Below: On 24th November 1981, RM19 (HT) has run around the block at Finsbury Park station on its way to its Tufnell Park terminus (actually Holloway garage) on route 19. Added interest in this photograph is provided by the Deltic diesel, probably 55008, on the bridge behind - these were in their final weeks of service at this time. Also, a Leyland National on route 236 is visible between the two. RMs and RMLs continued to operate route 19 until the end of March 2005, having replaced RTs on it in August 1972.

Quite an odd coincidence on 1st April 1986 is that of RM2002 (SW), registered ALM2B, working route 2B. It awaits the off at Golders Green Bus Station for Crystal Palace, retracing much of the first route (the 2) to be operated by the first RM over thirty years previously in February 1956. But by now, withdrawal of RMs is steadily proceeding, as shown by the Metrobus on the right, which had replaced them on route 260 in 1984. The 2B had gained RMs in October 1986, subsequently being upgraded to RML operation. In its last few years, it was renumbered as route 2, and converted to O.P.O. in January 1994.

Below: Next day, on 2nd April 1986, early-bodied RM24 (CF) approaches Mornington Crescent Station on route 24, which was usually RML-operated at this period. It converted to O.P.O. Titans at the end of October the same year. The route had originally received RMs in the autumn of 1963, but was chosen as one of the routes for the RML/XA tests two years later. Having the latter until May 1966, it was then RML-operated until crew DMs replaced them in October 1975. Needless to say, these were a disaster and were swapped with route 18's RMLs in April 1979.

ROYAL ROUTEMASTERS

Not long after the last of the 1970s all-over advertisement RMs had run, it was decided to adorn 25 RMs in silver livery to commemorate H.M. Queen Elizabeth II's Silver Jubilee in 1977. Each RM was sponsored by an advertiser, for whom all external and internal adverts were dedicated. Random RMs going through Aldenham overhaul were chosen, and all temporarily renumbered SRM1-25 for the duration of the project. On Easter Sunday, 10th April 1977, all were unveiled at the Easter Parade in Battersea Park, and then did a tour around Central London. This view sees SRM7, alias RM1871, in the procession on Albert Embankment.

Two days later, SRM11 (PM), otherwise RM1910, turns right from Bridge Street into Parliament Street on Tuesday, 12th April 1977, their first weekday in service. The buses were allocated to routes serving Central London tourist attractions, of which 'Big Ben' on the right is one of the most obvious, and rotated to different routes during the summer.

Some of the RMs involved found themselves on Sunday-only routes, as SRM25/RM1850 (NX) has on 17th April 1977. It crosses Waterloo Bridge on the Sunday 1A, heading for Greenwich Church, another well-known tourist spot with the Cutty Sark and the Maritime Museum. Just visible in the distance on the left is another of the 25 SRMs, SRM13/RM1648 on the same route.

Above: Some time before the celebrations began, prototype RM2 had been adorned in Silver Jubilee livery as a test vehicle. It was seldom seen outside Chiswick Works at this period, but on 26th July 1977, runs west along Victoria Street on trade plates. Standard RM442 was also so adorned for a press launch, but not used in this guise in service.

Right: The mean streets of North Kensington, where the Notting Hill Carnival had recently been marred by serious rioting and attacks on the Police, were certainly not tourist spots in 1977, but of course SRMs reached them on the outer ends of routes 7 and 52. SRM18/RM1906 (X) heads for Tottenham Court Road at Ladbroke Grove Station on 20th October 1977; the advertisements on the right add to the 'period' atmosphere.

Although a couple took part in the 1977 Lord Mayor's Show two days later, and some lasted almost to the end of the month, on 10th November 1977, SRM9/RM1907 is one of several at Aldenham Works waiting to be repainted back into red livery. Forty years later, RM1650 is preserved as 'SRM3' but carries a different body to that the real SRM3 had, and in any case is one of the TfL 'returnee' RMs refurbished with awful hopper windows, as will be illustrated later in these pages.

For the wedding of Prince Charles and Lady Diana Spencer in July 1981, a number of RMs were adorned in a special purple and grey livery, again featuring various advertisers' wares.

The pilot vehicle for this was RM490, which was exhibited at the very first North Weald Bus Rally on 31st May 1981. However, it never operated in this condition.

Most of the RMs actually operated in this livery were examples that were twenty or more years old and having their fourth overhauls. On 7th July 1981, RM520 (N) passes Hyde Park Corner Station in the late evening sunshine. I particularly remember on this occasion how a well-known, veteran bus photographer had been waiting patiently here to catch a three-quarter offside view of this bus on its stop. His pictures always had to be 'just so', but unfortunately for him, it pulled up a little too far beyond its stop, meaning part of its front was in shadow. Therefore he didn't photograph it! It was lucky for me that I took my shot before it stopped there! These buses were not only allocated to specific routes, but also to specific duties on them, thus explaining our long wait for this one.

Considering there were only eight 'Royal Wedding RMs', it was very unusual to see two in service together, but on 20th July 1981, RM595 (WL) which is turning short just across Westminster Bridge on route 12 passes one of its fellows on route 53 outside County Hall.

Illustrating the rear-end treatment of the Royal Wedding RMs, which were dressed up to look like wedding gift parcels, RM519 (X) has unusually been allocated to suburban route 187, instead of the central London 7 it was intended to work, on 5th September 1981. For some reason, the advertising space on its back has been left blank as it heads along Park Parade, Harlesden.

A number of RMs and RMLs were adorned in a special gold livery for the Queen's Golden Jubilee in 2002. Once again these were operated on routes serving the City and West End and also had dedicated advertising for various firms, but on 23rd March 2002, RM6 (BN) has yet to have its advertisements applied when leaving route 159's Marble Arch terminus for Streatham. The badly painted front registration plate and dented dome all bear testament to the deterioration in standards since the Silver Jubilee RMs of 25 years earlier, not least thanks to the closure of Aldenham Works by the Thatcher regime's London Regional Transport quango in 1986.

Whether by accident or design, RM1650 (X) which had masqueraded as SRM3 in 1977, was also chosen as a Golden Jubilee RM. However, it was in fact an entirely different vehicle, which in the meantime had been sold and seen service in Blackpool and Reading before being acquired in 2000 by TfL and refurbished by Marshall of Cambridge. In this view, it approaches Bank Station on 27th May 2002 on the new route 23 which had replaced the western section of route 15 almost ten years previously. As this book is being finalised in early October 2017, this route has been cut back from Liverpool Street to Aldwych, no longer serving the City.

OTHER SPECIAL LIVERIES

In the spring of 1979, a dozen RMs were adorned in a dark green and yellow livery approximating that of George's Shillibeer's omnibuses, the 150th anniversary of which they were commemorating. As with the SRMs, RM2 had been used as a pilot. On 2nd March 1979, they are lined up outside the City Guildhall for a press launch, three of the RMs are out of the picture on the right. However new DM 2646, last of this awful type to be built, also carries the livery: 'unlucky thirteen' indeed, and I wonder whether this was done merely for Schadenfreude, considering that although the RMs were some of the last built, and were going through their second overhauls, were fourteen years old!

On 4th March 1979, just two days after the launch, a gleaming RM2208 (WW) passes West Ham Park on its way from Chingford to North Woolwich on trolleybus replacement route 69. The Shillibeer-liveried RMs also carried adverts inside and out for various companies, and were rotated around various routes during the year. However, unlike the SRMs, they worked on routes that did not serve central London. This RM is now smartly restored in this livery.

Concurrent with the appearance of the Shillibeer RMs, a further batch of those in the RM21/2200 series having their second overhauls were adorned for a special 'Shoplinker' service, aimed as the name suggests at shoppers in the West End. On 18th March 1969, two of them, RM2188 and 2146 are posed for a press launch in Oxford Street. Their livery was normal LT red below the lower-deck windows and on the roof, and yellow on the rest of the bodywork. Obviously, they did not carry the rather inane protrusions seen here when in service!

On Easter Saturday, 14th April 1979, RM59 (SW) heads along Kensington High Street. This was the odd one out amongst the Shoplinkers being, numerically at least, older than the others on the service. It also had an unique style of very distinctive in-house London Transport external advertising, as this view clearly shows. And who in 1979 could foresee that the famous Woolworth's stores, like the one on the left, would be defunct some 35 years later?

In outer north-west London, RM2142 (HD) is at Yeading, White Hart when loading up on route 140 on Easter Monday, 16th April 1979. As may be seen it advertises North Thames Gas, then a nationalised concern which would be privatised thanks to the Thatcher regime which came to power just over a fortnight after this picture was taken! And route 140, which had only gained RMs in July 1978 sixteen years after it should have done originally, lost them in April 1983 when it converted to Metrobus operation.

The Shoplinker RMs were based at Stockwell Garage, where nine of them (with RM2159 and RM2172 nearest the camera) make an impressive line-up beneath the garage's equally impressive vast concrete roof span. The date is also Easter Monday, 1979 and the coaches on the right are vehicles laying over on overnight services between Scotland and Victoria.

On a route I had conducted from nearby Clapton Garage in 1974/75, the 22, RM2186 (B) turns right from Mare Street into Graham Road, Hackney on 13th May 1979. A DMS follows on route 22A, which at the time ran from Clapton Park Estate to Wapping, paralleling the 22 from Homerton to Shoreditch. The 22 was withdrawn north of Piccadilly Circus in February 1990, but its surviving section retained Routemasters until July 2005.

On the same day, RM2159 (SW) turns from Lower Regent Street into Piccadilly on the Shoplinker service's two-way loop working. Oddly, the route did not have a route number and instead had '30p', indicating its flat-fare, shown where that would normally be. This caused confusion on the Marble Arch to Knightsbridge section of the route where the real route 30 also ran, so was later discontinued.

This view of RM2130 (NB) at the Chessington Zoo terminus of route 65 on 16th May 1979 illustrates the application of Shillibeer livery to the rear of the RMs. There were some very minor differences in its application between the vehicles, which unfortunately are difficult to discern in mono photographs. Route 65 would retain RMs until the summer of 1985 when it converted to crew Metrobus, though a small Sunday allocation of Hanwell RMLs survived into early 1986.

The Shoplinker service was not a success, and was withdrawn after six months. On its last day, 28th September 1979, RM2207 (SW), devoid of any route number display, is almost empty when running through Queens Gate, Kensington. It was one of a couple that had wrap-round advertisements which were retained after it was repainted into standard red livery.

Unlike the SRMs, Shillibeer RMs finished up with in-house London Transport advertising once their sponsors' contracts were up, some lasting a few weeks into 1980. They also strayed onto routes they had not been intended to work, thus as dusk falls on 14th February 1980, RM2160 (AR) is working route 41 when turning from Turnpike Lane into Green Lanes. Of note is a new, unpainted pink panel in front of its offside rear wheel, which has been left unpainted as the RM is imminently due to go to Aldenham for repaint into red. The 41 converted to Metrobus OPO in November 1985.

Just one Routemaster was adorned in a special gold livery to commemorate London Transport's Golden Jubilee in 1983. This was RM1983 (V) which operated on a number of Central London routes during that summer. It approaches Hammersmith Broadway on route 27 on 25th June 1983. Route 27 gained RMs daily in June 1970, and converted to OPO in October 1986.

Four other RMs, however - RM8 (SP), RM17 (AC), RM1933 (CF) and RM2116 (AP) - were adorned in an approximation of 1933 'General' Livery to mark the event. On 15th October 1983, they are paraded at a special film show and rally at Muswell Hill Odeon. Only a cursory glance will immediately show that each has a minor variation in livery.

RM89 (GM) was one of two also adorned in an approximation of 'General' livery at Victoria, Gillingham Street Garage in the late 1980s. On 10th December 1989, it works a private hire to the Grays State Cinema (actually for my old friend Dominic West' 30th birthday) when loading up at Euston Square. The Grey Green vehicle on the left typifies this era, when the L.R.T. quango was tendering routes out to all and sundry, with buses in greys, greens, blues and yellows running London bus routes throughout the system.

The next batch of RMs to have special liveries was those working route 159, which somewhat absurdly was put up for tender and won by London Buses' subsidiary South London, starting operation in the spring of 1994 shortly before privatisation. In June 1994, RM6 (BN) heads south at Oxford Circus bearing the 159's smart red and cream livery, somewhat reminiscent of that once carried by Brighton, Hove and District buses, complete with full route-branding, but still also bearing the London Buses' bullseye logo.

Inevitably, RMs in '159' livery strayed onto Brixton Garage's other crew route, the 137. In August 1994, low-bodied RM275 (BN) has done so, though admittedly does not yet have route-branding for the 159. The London Buses' logo is also absent. It stands at the 137's John Princes Street terminus. Conversely, RMLs from Brixton Garage in normal livery worked on the 159, several of whose RM allocation also retained this. Indeed a mixture of RMs and RMLs worked the route until the very end in December 2005.

By accident or design, the second-lowest numbered RM, RM6 which had also regained its original body on last overhaul, and the highest-numbered one, RM2217 were both among the 159's customised RMs. They are exhibited here at the North Weald Bus Rally on 25th June 1995. From early 1997 onwards, the special livery was abandoned and the RMs were painted in standard red livery again, although at that time, no one could ever have guessed the route would remain Routemaster-operated until December 2005!

An oddity to appear in the summer of 2004 was RM25 (B) adorned in this peculiar livery commemorating Great Northern Tramways. On 18th March 2005, it departs from route 19's ramshackle base in Hester Road, Battersea a fortnight before the route converted to O.P.O. The grotesque new building on the left occupies the site where the original Battersea Garage once stood. This had only been rebuilt in the mid-1970s, but was closed by the L.R.T. regime in November 1985, though used for a few months after that for the Round London Sightseeing Tour.

RM1933, which along with RM1983 had been sold to Kelvin Scottish for use in the Glasgow area in the mid-1980s, was reacquired for London use by TfL, and re-entered service on route 13 in the summer of 2001. Following that route's O.P.O. conversion in October 2005, it was selected as one of the handful of RMs retained for route 15's 'heritage' service. In 2008, it was adorned in this adaptation of West Ham Tramways' livery to commemorate the 75th anniversary of London Transport, and crosses Ludgate Circus in April that year. Previously, it had again carried 'General' livery when working this service, but at the time of writing is red again.

RM ODDITIES

Although like the RTs before them, RMs were highly standardised, there were nevertheless a number of oddities amongst them over the years. One of the best known was RM738 (EM), which was fitted with this odd-looking radiator grille in an effort to lessen the loud engine noises made by RMs, especially when accelerating away from stops. On a gloomy February 3rd, 1968, it heads south past Finsbury Park on trolleybus replacement route 127, which was heavily cut back in September that year and withdrawn completely in January 1970. This RM retained this fitting when transferred to Abbey Wood Garage for route 180 later in 1968, but no others were fitted with such grilles - presumably it made no difference to the noisy RMs!

By 9th May 1978, RMs with full-depth ventilator grilles beneath their front blind displays were a thing of the past, even those few overhauled like this in 1971. However, for some reason, RM833 (AK) retained this feature long after all others had lost it and was thus unique when caught heading south along Whitehall, bound for its home garage on what would be the last RM route of all.

Over the years, a handful of Routemaster bodies (both RM and RML type) which had originally had opening front upper-deck windows were rebuilt after accidents with non-opening front windows. RM1220 (SW) has one such body when working route 37 along The Avenue, Clapham Common on 10th May 1980. A close look at the front dome shows that it does not have the ventilator slat as fitted to RMs originally built with non-opening front upper-deck windows, thereby limiting its ventilation on a warm day as it appears to be here! This was one of the RMs that had supplemented route 37's RMLs on Saturdays since it gained them in the summer of 1966. It converted to OPO twenty years after that.

Another oddity, window-wise, at this period was RM679 (AK). It was rebuilt after an accident with the second window from the back on its offside upper-deck as an opener, rather than the standard arrangement of the second, third and fourth upper-deck offside windows being openers. This anomaly is clearly evident in this view of it in Oxford Street on route 159 on 22nd September 1980. No one could then have imagined that this route would keep RMs for more than a quarter of a century afterwards, and end up as London's last all-Routemaster route!

An oddity based at Tottenham garage during 1985 was RM1877, which had been equipped with a wrap-round 'tween-decks advertisement promoting bus adverts. Here on 3rd July 1985, it passes the monstrous County Hall Island Block on its way from Forest Hill to Bruce Grove. Route 171 was withdrawn north of Islington Green six months later, then converted to O.P.O. in August 1986.

On New Year's Eve, 1973, the upper deck of RM1368 was destroyed, perhaps by arsonists, in Tottenham Garage. However instead of being scrapped, it was adopted as the 'Chiswick Experimental' RM and converted to single-deck, releasing the previously long-term incumbent in that role, RM8 for service. It is still at Chiswick on 9th May 1986, and has subsequently been preserved.

RM931 (AD) was a real oddity in that it had been out of service for eight years between 1973 and 1981, initially owing to the spare parts shortage of the mid-1970s. It was gradually robbed of virtually all mechanical parts, and some body parts too, and ended up being dumped at the rear of Bexleyheath garage - which never operated RMs - alongside withdrawn RTs. However, it was saved from the scrapyard by the abysmal performance of the DMSs, which forced London Transport to keep its Routemasters, and put back together again and overhauled at Aldenham in 1981. This view sees it at Spouters Corner, Wood Green on 15th July 1986. It would also be returned to London in 2000, and finished up on route 13 five years later. Of note are the 'route-branding' posters on the front of the RM, a current fad of the period. Also of note are the buildings behind the bus-stop on the right - the green and white structure was a tram shelter built in the early 1930s, with inspector's hut and public conveniences attached, in conjunction with the tube station seen behind it. Sadly, it was demolished in the late 1990s, but Chas Holden's splendid station still, of course, remains.

An oddity produced by the Aldenham overhaul system was RM796 (WD), which was outshopped on its final overhaul with a much later body with an offside illuminated advertisement panel. Apart from the pilot RM of this type, RM1577 illustrated earlier in this book, all such vehicles were otherwise numbered in the RM19/20/2100s. This view finds it in Dalston Lane working route 22 from Wandsworth Garage on 30th December 1986. The 22's traditional allocation at Battersea Garage had been transferred there when that garage closed in November 1985, in July 1987, Wandsworth itself was closed, and the 22 again reallocated to Putney. Then in November 1987, the route was cut back to Bloomsbury during the week, so its RMs would no longer serve the Dalston area! It was further cut back to Piccadilly Circus in February 1990. However, it would eventually retain Routemasters until July 2005.

For several years in the 1980s, early-bodied RM45 was used as a training vehicle to acquaint drivers with radio equipment used for route control. This view finds it passing Mornington Crescent Station on 27th April 1987. It was subsequently sold to Strathtay Scottish, and when they had finished with it, it found its way to Reading Main Line in the mid-1990s. Then, after their operation ceased, it was bought back by Transport for London, refurbished and returned to service on 1st September 2001 on route 13, where it remained until that route's O.P.O. conversion in October 2005. An oddity indeed!

On my local route 29, RM339 (AD) is an oddity in having a black 'skirt' which is clearly visible as it calls at the stop at the junction of Green Lanes and Hedge Lane, Palmers Green, near my home, on 28th June 1988. This was an intended new livery for Leaside District buses as a prelude to privatisation, though in the event only this RM, an RML and a few Metrobuses ever received it. Route 29 converted to O.P.O. Metrobus in November 1988.

Similarly, RM1666 (Q) gained a grey skirt upon repaint at this period. On 12th August 1988, it heads for home along Penge High Street and would remain unique. The very battered front dome illustrates how shoddy RMs were getting at this period, having not been repaired when it was repainted, as it would have been when Aldenham Works was still open. Route 12 retained RMs and RMLs until they were replaced by bendibuses in November 2004, but by that time it had been withdrawn south of Dulwich.

Route 13 was tendered out to BTS of Borehamwood in December 1993, bizarrely using refurbished RMLs leased to them by London Buses Ltd. In the summer of 1994, the operator bought RM104, which had by then operated in Scotland for a few years, and had it refurbished to work as a spare on the route. On 21st July 1994, it has turned short and stands in Waterloo Place. Its platform provides a convenient seat for its crew to sit on enjoying the sunshine. The RM had been re-registered when operating for Clydeside Scottish in the Glasgow area, and ironically others similarly treated would work route 13 in its final years of crew operation, 2001-2005.

A real oddity to appear in the last couple of years of London Central and London General RM operation was RM2051 (Q). Not only did it have no air intake grille below its front blind box, as graphically illustrated here, it was also re-registered DGW128B from ALM51B as well as being fitted with hopper windows. This was because many of the feral youths riding on RMs on the southern sections of routes 12 and 36 found great pleasure in aiming missiles from them at pedestrians in the street! On Bank Holiday Monday, 30th August 2004, this RM passes Marble Arch on the special 12X service for the Notting Hill Carnival. This was the last time this, and the similar 36X operated, since both the 12 and 36 had converted to O.P.O. by the time of the next one.

SHORT-LIVED RM WORKINGS

Route 8B was introduced with RMs on 7th September 1968, effectively replacing RTL-operated route 60 between Cricklewood Garage and Oxford Circus, but then continuing to Tottenham Court Road Station (or Bloomsbury in rush hours) rather than Waterloo as the 60 had. On 20th May 1970, RM613 (W) - which is now, numerically, a well-known preserved RM frequently seen in and around London today - heads west along Oxford Street. Route 8B was withdrawn three weeks later.

A very short-lived and seldom photographed RM working was that of the Saturday-only 159A, on which they replaced RTs in June 1970, but was withdrawn at the end of October the same year. On 26th September 1970, RM642 (Q) heads through Cavendish Square five weeks before the route was discontinued. RM642 also survives in preservation today.

Also operated by Cricklewood Garage, route 32 was introduced with RMs in June 1970, replacing the southern section of route 142 and running between Edgware Station and Kilburn Park Station. However, just under nine months later, some of the first O.M.O. DMSs replaced RMs on this route. On 6th March 1971, a week before this happened, RM1711 (W) sets off from the stand at the latter point leaving RM1013 (W) behind.

Even more short-lived was RM operation on route 124 and its Sunday variant the 124A. RMs replaced RTs in July 1971, but were themselves replaced by O.M.O. DMSs in January 1972. On 9th August 1971, RM488 (TL) passes Welling Corner heading for its terminus at nearby Springfield Road. Of note is the fact that this RM has a full-depth ventilator grille (as originally fitted) beneath its front blind display. For some reason, a number of RMs had been overhauled retaining this feature at this period.

One of the shortest-lived RM workings of all was that of the new route 46, which was introduced in January 1972, localising the Hampstead Heath to Farringdon Street portion of route 45, which in turn had replaced part of the 513/613 trolleybus routes eleven years before. On 18th March 1972, RM389 (CF) passes the famous Gamages department store in High Holborn, nearing its southern terminus. The route converted to DMS O.M.O. in June that year.

On 18th June 1973, RM313 (T) passes one of its stablemates on new route 269 at Chingford Mount, Prince Albert as an MBS rattles its way towards Walthamstow on route W21. This route had been introduced two days earlier to replace the northern sections of routes 69 and 262 between Walthamstow and Chingford, overlapping the 69 as far as Leyton, Downsell Road. However, at the end of January 1976, the route was withdrawn and the 69 reinstated to Chingford Station. Curiously, exactly five years later, the 69 was again cut back (this time only to Chingford Mount) and a new route DMS O.P.O. route 97 introduced running between Chingford Station and Leyton, Downsell Road - exactly as the 269 had. Presumably it was not a coincidence that this used the same number as tram route 97 which had traversed the same route between Chingford Mount and Leyton before being replaced by the 697 trolleybus before the war!

Perhaps the shortest-lived scheduled RM operation of all was that on route 51A. It gradually converted to RM operation during January 1977, using RMs displaced by MDs from route 53, but was withdrawn on 21st May that year when the associated 51 converted to O.P.O. DMS. Four days before that happened, RM604 (SP) calls at Welling Post Office working one of the 51A's rush hour journeys that were extended from Woolwich to Charlton Station. A sticker on the bus stop flag warns of the impending route changes.

Another route in south east London on which full RM operated was short-lived was the 228. Although it had been RM-operated on Saturdays since March 1975 (using buses from the 21's allocation), it did not convert from RT to RM until May 1977. Only eight months later, in January 1978, it converted in turn to DMS O.P.O. This busy scene on 27th September 1977 sees an apparently empty RM1602 (SP) at Eltham Church, nearing the end of its short journey from Chislehurst.

Although RMs occasionally substituted for crew DMs on tram replacement route 168 after they replaced its RTs in September 1975, it was not until December 1980 that they fully operated the route. Just after that happened, RM1736 (SW) has turned short at Vauxhall Station on Christmas Eve, 24th December 1980. Their operation was very short-lived indeed, since the route was withdrawn only four months later and replaced by alterations to route 77A, which already duplicated much of it.

Probably to lessen the shock of mass O.P.O. conversions and consequent RM withdrawals - not to mention conductor redundancies - following the 'Law Lords" service cuts of 4th September 1982, some new routes were introduced with RM operation as an interim measure. One was the 225, which replaced route 86 between Limehouse and Bow, and route 25 between Ilford and Becontree Heath as well as duplicating both between Bow and Ilford. A fortnight after its introduction, RM716 (WH) passes the Merry Fiddlers pub at Becontree on its way west on 16th September 1982. However, O.P.O. Titans replaced its RMs just over seven months later.

Another such route was the 60, replacing the northern end of route 130 between South Croydon Garage and Streatham Garage. Effectively, the RMs replaced crew DMs, since the 130 had received these to replace RMLs in March 1975. Sadly, it too was not to last as the new 60 also converted to O.P.O., this time using DMSs, in April 1983. A fortnight before that happened, RM1948 (TC) passes Thornton Heath Pond heading for home on 9th April. This RM had recently been overhauled with the body originally on RM2217 - the last 64-seat RM built.

Above: New route 261 replaced parts of route 94, and was RM-operated for the same short timespan as route 60, somewhat oddly converting to single-deck LS O.P.O. in April 1983. On 21st of that month, its penultimate day of RM operation, RM574 (TB) passes through Farnborough Common. The bus has been partially restored to its original 1960 appearance by staff at Bromley Garage at a time when many RMs were adopted by staff as 'showbuses', and taken to bus rallies and so on.

Right: Other sections of the withdrawn 94 were replaced by new route 208, also initially RM-operated. On 15th June 1983, RM288 (TL) heads along Rotherhithe New Road towards Surrey Docks Station, to which the route was extended during Saturday shopping hours. This route retained RMs somewhat longer than the 69, 225 and 261, losing them in June 1984.

The last new Routemaster-operated route of all was the 390, which replaced the northern end of route 10 at the end of January 2003. Mainly RML-operated, a few RMs were also used until the route converted to O.P.O. in September 2004, thus also making it a short-lived working. Most of its time, it operated from Holloway Garage's outstation in York Way, Kings Cross. On 31st July 2004, five weeks before its O.P.O. conversion, RM1971 (KC) has just passed its base and has as a backdrop the former York Road Piccadilly Line station, which had closed in 1932.

FIRES AND MISHAPS

In all their years at London's service, only three Routemasters were destroyed by fire when actually out in service. The first, RM1768 at Marble Arch in July 1966 is well-known. The second was RM500 (HT) which caught fire when working route 143 in East Finchley, and the remains of the vehicle were towed back to Highgate garage in whose depths it is hidden on 10th January 1968, a couple of days afterwards. Because two extra 'float' RM bodies had been built to facilitate their overhauls, both this and the first victim were returned to service utilising the extra bodies, but an RML that caught fire in 2002 was not so lucky - no spare RML bodies existed and, besides, by then 'the writing was on the wall' for them.

Left: A remarkable sight in the Old Kent Road as dusk falls on 30th January 1971 is that of RM456 (NX) with a smashed front dome, still carrying passengers! They appear to be a school party for which the bus has operated a private hire. The most likely cause of the damage is one of the low bridges beneath the Southern Region lines that radiate from London Bridge Station, and no doubt a quick visit to Aldenham remedied things. However, the driver may well have had some awkward questions to answer when he got back to New Cross Garage!

Below: RM304 sustained this severe damage when rammed on its offside by, of all things, a milk tanker when working night route N97 at Fulham Broadway in the autumn of 1971. Taken to Aldenham and assessed for repair, it was in the event withdrawn as, at the time, replacement of RMs was expected to begin in around four or five years' time. Although its lower deck and cab area were seriously distorted, as well as its front sub-frame, the bus could obviously have been rebuilt using parts salvaged from three others damaged by fire a few months later, as shown below. This view shows RM304 parked outside Aldenham Works on 4th October 1972 with various scrap RTs. Various undamaged parts of it were re-used, notably its roof which went to another Routemaster which had been deroofed by a low bridge.

In the spring of 1972, arsonists broke into Peckham garage and set fire to RM1659, the remains of which are also seen in company with defunct RTs outside Aldenham Works on 4th October that year. Not surprisingly, it was written off.

Unfortunately, two other RMs standing beside RM1659 were badly damaged too. RM1447 was standing to its offside and suffered severe damage to its own nearside, as illustrated here. The bus in front of it is RM1268, which had less serious damage to its offside as it was parked to the nearside of the stricken RM1659. Both of these too were written off, even though at least one 'good' RM could probably have been salvaged using the nearside of RM1268 and the offside of RM1447, along with various spares no doubt kept at Aldenham! At the time, it was still thought that RM withdrawals would begin in a few years' time anyway, not ten years later as in fact happened in the end.

On 12th May 1973, RM2035 (GM) has come to grief, sustaining a nasty dent to its front dome and a smashed nearside wing. It is parked in the yard of its home garage, Victoria Gillingham Street, where also RMs from other garages which had had accidents in central London were often parked before retrieval. In all probability, this RM will have to go to Aldenham for repairs.

Until the very end, the sight of a broken-down Routemaster at the roadside in London was a rare one, but of course such things did happen. On 16th October 1974, RM1171 (AR) has let the side down by breaking down in Oxford Street whilst working route 73 in the evening rush hour. A group of fitters, along with a Thames Trader breakdown truck, have been called out to attend to it and, in the event, had to tow it home to Tottenham Garage. To add insult to injury, the bus had only just come out of overhaul at Aldenham Works - its gleaming 'innards' may just be discerned beneath its raised bonnet!

During the autumn of 1979, a fire engine crashed into RM1879 (AL) when it was working route 49 in South Kensington, causing it to overturn. Unlike the unfortunate RM304, however, it was only slightly damaged and on 2nd November 1978 has been given new external panels where appropriate, and awaits repaint at Aldenham Works. It went on to have another overhaul there, ending up with a low-numbered body.

Parked outside Aldenham Works too on 25th September 1983, RM840 has suffered very serious front-end damage when working from Wandsworth Garage, and it is to be hoped its driver was not seriously injured. However, it was repaired at Aldenham, later seeing service at Edmonton Garage.

London Transport's ill-fated DMSs were intended not only to replace the remaining RTs when introduced at the beginning of 1971, but also, eventually, the RMs. Indeed, the very first ones into service did so, on routes 95, 220 and 271, although at that stage, the Routemasters they replaced were moved on to replace RTs elsewhere. Between 1973 and 1975, many DM-types replaced RMs and RMLs (and some RTs) as crew-operated vehicles, but just like their O.P.O. equivalents, proved a disaster in service. Therefore, towards the end of the 1970s, RMs were returned to routes where DMs or DMSs had replaced them. Much to my pleasure, the first route to benefit was the 29, which had converted to crew DM in December 1975. On its first day of the RMs' return, 19th March 1977, RM985 (HT) loads up at Wood Green, Spouter's Corner. The route was also diverted and extended to Enfield to replace route 123 (which converted to DMS O.P.O. the same day), but the 29's RM conversion was at the expense of route 141 which exchanged its RMs for the 29s DMs, in fact this RM is still showing an NX garage code, having been transferred from New Cross to Holloway. I lived just around the corner from the location shown at the time; in fact the lady standing by the bus stop is my wife Felicity.

he first one-man-operated route to benefit from regaining RMs was the Sunday 279A, which had been introduced with DMSs in March 1973. With the nter-war Woodberry Down Estate as a backdrop, RM1679 (EM) approaches Manor House Station on the first day of their return, 29th October 1978.

More drastic was the return of RMs daily to busy inner-suburban route 106, on which DMSs had been a complete disaster since they replaced RMs originally in July 1972, not least when one shuddered to a halt abruptly and catapulted a lady who had stood up to alight from the front upper-deck seats through its flimsy front windows and into the street below! On their second day in service, 1st April 1979, newly-overhauled RM1291 (AR) stands at Finsbury Park, Plimsoll Road terminus, where the route terminated on Sundays instead of at the station. The low building beside the RM is a purpose-built LT canteen, which had replaced a canteen trailer here some twenty years previously. Sadly, route 106 reverted to O.P.O., albeit with Titans, amid the 'Law Lords' cuts of September 1982; the terminus here was abandoned in early 1985 when Finsbury Park, Station Place, bus station was enlarged. Meanwhile, some DMSs had perished in the Yorkshire scrapyards early in 1979, even before the last RTs had been withdrawn!

In 1976/77, RMs had been replaced by the experimental MD class, working as crew buses, on the 36 group of routes and the 63 at Peckham Garage, and the 53 at New Cross. Although not as disastrous as the DMSs, the MDs were heavy on fuel and also suffered corrosion problems, therefore were redeployed to O.P.O. routes in south east London and RMs returned to their original routes. On 10th February 1980, RM1444 (PM) passes Ladywell Baths in Lewisham High Street on route 36B, to which, numerically, it had been new in early 1963. Although by then rationalised to be route 36 only, RMs remained working the 36 group until January 2005.

Trunk route 207, running the length of the Uxbridge Road, had replaced the 607 trolleybus in November 1960 using RMs, and received RMLs seven years later. It was converted to crew DM operation in the spring of 1976 but as usual, these were not a success. The route was gradually converted to Routemaster operation in the latter half of 1980, at first using a mixture of RMs and RMLs, and completed thanks to the overhauling of the remaining ex-London Country RMLs. On 20th August 1980, low-bodied RM730 passes through Ealing Common on a short working to Acton High Street. The 207 converted to Metrobus O.P.O. in March 1987.

As with the 36 group of routes illustrated earlier, route 53 converted back from MD to RM operation early in 1981. On 6th May 1981, RM707 (NX) heads a cluster of Routemasters at Great Portland Street Station in the evening rush hour. The route converted to O.P.O. in January 1988.

n common with that of the 106, O.P.O. DMS operation on route 55, which had received them to replace RTs at the end of October 1972, was a isaster, therefore it was reconverted to crew RM operation at the end of January 1981. On 7th May 1981, RM716 (T) heads south along Hoe Street, Valthamstow bound for Victoria. The route was extended there from Bloomsbury upon reversion to RM working to supplement the 38. Later pgraded to RML, it converted to Titan O.P.O. in June 1987.

On the same day the previous picture was taken, RM56 (WH) passes East Ham Town Hall on its way from Waterloo to Becontree Heath. The 5 had been one of the first routes to use RMs in trolleybus replacement, in November 1959 and, numerically, this RM had worked it when new. Upgraded to RMLs in early 1966, it too suffered DMS conversion in April 1971, but ten years later was also reverted to RM operation. Subsequently receiving RMLs again, it converted to Titan operation in November 1985.

Next day, 8th May 1981, RM1397 (WL) terminates at Kings Cross Station in the evening rush hour. This route had been converted to crew DM from Walworth Garage in March 1975, when it ran all the way from South Kensington via a very circuitous route encompassing Battersea, Clapham, Stockwell, Brixton, Camberwell, Elephant & Castle, Blackfriars and Holborn to Kings Cross. In October 1978, it was extended from Kings Cross via Caledonian Road and Holloway Road replacing route 17 (which it had overlapped between Camberwell and Kings Cross) and a Holloway allocation added. DMs replaced RMs from both garages in the spring of 1981, but the route converted to O.P.O. in August 1985 when it was cut back to Kings Cross again from the north.

Tram replacement route 172 was shared between Holloway and Camberwell Garages and had converted from RT to crew DM working in August 1975. It too gained RMs, which had hitherto only been scheduled to work it at weekends, in the spring of 1981. On 3rd June 1981, low-bodied RM115 (HT) calls at Addington Street, Waterloo working short to Brixton. The DM behind is substituting for an RM on route 53, also recently reverted to the type. In September 1982, route 172 was rerouted at Westminster to run to Kings Cross via Aldwych, and its Holloway allocation withdrawn. The route itself followed in August 1985.

Above: Also in the spring of 1981, a number of other routes based at Holloway Garage, which had received crew DMs in 1975, were converted to RM operation. One was route 4, which had only been scheduled for them on Saturdays hitherto otherwise being RT-worked. On 28th July 1981, RM1221 (HT) is about to be overtaken by RM62 (CT) on route 22 on the one-way system at St. Paul's Station.

Right: Pioneer RML-operated route 104 had also converted to crew DM in 1975 and was reverted to Routemaster operation in 1981. On 8th September that year, early-bodied RM98 (HT) passes through the Holloway, Nag's Head shopping centre. Both bodily and numerically, this RM is some two years older than the RMLs that had replaced trolleybuses on this route nearly twenty years before. Sadly, route 104 converted to O.P.O. as a result of the cuts of September 1982, and was withdrawn just under three years later. Ironically, today route 263 covers most of its original routeing, from Barnet to Highbury Corner.

Having exchanged its RMs with route 29s DMs in March 1977, route 141 eventually regained RMs five years later. On 1st June 1982, RM298 (NX) heads north along St. George's Road, Lambeth working its southern portion, which usually ran between Grove Park and Newington Green, whereas the northern section ran from Moorgate to Wood Green. Unfortunately, the route converted to O.P.O. early in 1985. Today, RM298 forms part of The London Bus Company's heritage fleet.

Covering much of the same route (between Highgate Station and Moorgate) as the 104, route 43 was another that had gained crew DMs early in 1975. Upon the 'Law Lords' cuts of 4th September 1982, there were plenty of RMs to replace them - which they did! On the first day of their return, RM1709 (MH) heads south past Holloway Road Station as an Inter-City express speeds across the bridge on the East Coast Main Line. The 43 subsequently gained RMLs, and was converted to Metrobus OPO in July 1987.

On the same day, route 134 also reverted to RM operation, having been the very first route to have crew worked DM-types foisted on it, in the autumn of 1973. On 21st April 1983, early-bodied RM784 (PB) speeds north up the Great North Road just south of Potters Bar, to which garage RMs returned for only seven and a half months - two days after this picture was taken, they were removed from it again, since the 134 was cut back to Barnet Church and replaced on the section seen here by new OPO route 234. Was it really worth bothering to return RMs to Potters Bar, which involved type-training and the production of new blinds for their RMs?

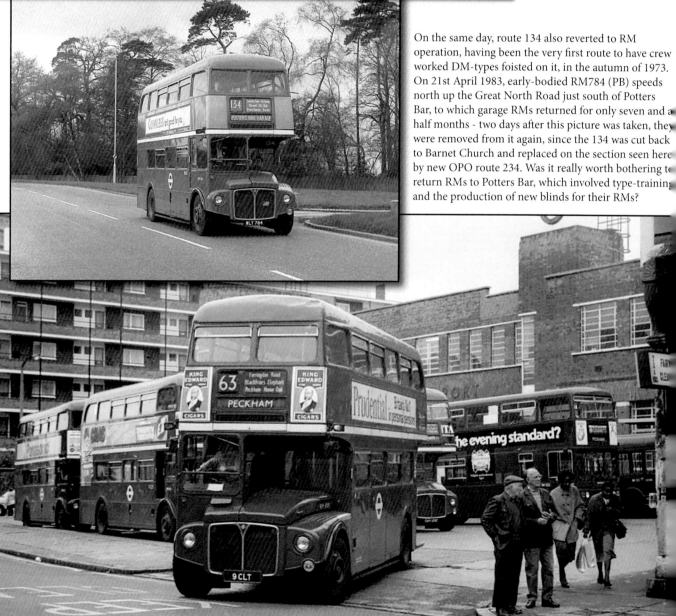

Route 63 was also reverted to RM operation on 4th September 1982, being the last MD-operated route to do so. Their return lasted until early November 1985, when OPO Titans took over. On its last day of crew operation, 2nd November 1985, RM1009 (PM) sets off from the small bus station in front of its home garage, its driver having failed to change the destination blind. The splendid LT garage, built in the early post-war years, seen in the background was closed in the spring of 1994 by the L.R.T. regime and its site sold off and built upon by a supermarket. However a larger bus station at least was provided here

SEE THE SIGHTS BY RM!

Early in 1986, some of the many withdrawn RMs now stored at the former Southall Works were selected for refurbishment for use on London Transport's Round London Sightseeing Tour. RMs had worked the tour in the early 1960s, but latterly DMSs and then Metrobuses had been used. Ironically, much of the work done on them was carried out at Loughton Garage, which had never operated RMs and never would, since it closed in May 1986 due to route tender losses. On 22nd March 1986, RM450 is one of a group standing outside Loughton's modern maintenance block, itself a 'mini-Aldenham', awaiting commissioning.

Right: The same day the previous picture was taken, the first RMs entered service on the tour, now renamed 'The Original London Sightseeing Tour'. The RMs were adorned in their original 1950s livery with cream waistbands, gold fleetnames and fleet numbers, complete with the word 'Routemaster' on the cab-side above the latter, although retained more recent front grille arrangements. All this was in an effort to compete with various private companies operating similar tours. Battersea Garage, which had been closed in November 1985, was reopened to accommodate the tour buses, which also included some of the last surviving RCLs and a few RMAs. On its first day in such use, RM307 (B) crosses Lambeth Bridge.

Below: Several of the sightseeing RMs had early bodies with non-opening front upper-deck windows. These were initially retained, and one of them is RM1919 (B), one of the highest-numbered RMs to have been overhauled with these bodies, which passes beneath Waterloo Bridge also on 22nd March 1986. The blue coach on the left stands outside what had been the exit to Kingsway Tram Subway.

After they had been refurbished, some of the sightseeing RMs were cut down to open-top. They were also rebuilt with RCL-style front blindboxes. Several of these also had non-opening front windows, which they retained. On 28th June 1986, I have taken my two little girls, Felicity (left) and Margaret (right), to see the sights on RM281 (B) which stands at the OLST's Piccadilly Circus pick-up point in Haymarket, for which it had a dedicated stop, seen on the right.

The Sightseeing Routemasters were reallocated from Battersea to Wandsworth Garage after that had also been closed in July 1987. Two additional RMs were actually reacquired for it and added to the open-top fleet, whilst a couple of others were also equipped with an access in their centre for wheelchairs. One of these is RM450 (WD), which sets off from Tower Hill leaving two ex-LT DMSs on competing operators' services on the stand in September 1991.

As with the remainder of the London Buses' constituent fleets, the sightseeing operation was privatised, and on 18th July 1992, open-top RM752 (WD) turns into Regent Street bearing a new livery, and the name London Coaches, all LT 'bullseyes' having been removed. By this time, some of the RMs had been extended to become 'ERMs', as will be illustrated in a future volume in this series, and all were eventually operated by Arriva.

NEW ROUTES FOR OLD RMs

Until very late in the RMs' careers, new routes were introduced using them. One example was the 135, introduced in November 1987 to replace the northern section of route 137, running between Archway Station and Marble Arch. On 28th of that month, RM1988 (HT) heads south along Hampstead Road. The upper-case via blind is of note, also the RM's cream waistband. This was by now one of the few Leyland-engined RMs still in service. Route 135 converted to O.P.O. at the beginning of November 1988, thus making it another short-lived RM operation, and has subsequently disappeared.

New route 10 was introduced in August 1988, replacing the western section of the 73 between Hammersmith and Hyde Park Corner, and overlapping it as far as Kings Cross. It was RML-operated from Holloway and Shepherd's Bush Garages, and on 13th August 1988, soon after its introduction, RM2185 (S), one of a number of spare RMs helping out at RML garages, calls at Hammersmith, Butterwick on its way back to the latter garage. Route 10 was the first to lose Routemasters in their last years, converting to O.P.O. at the end of January 2003.

In March 1992, new route 139 was introduced to replace the northern section of the 159, which was withdrawn between Baker Street and West Hampstead. Some journeys continued beyond the latter point to Golders Green, supplementing the 28. On its first day, 13th March, RM1218 (CF) has just passed the three railway stations in West End Lane. Interestingly, the new route restored crew operation to Chalk Farm Garage, which had been all-O.P.O. since October 1986, and the RMs used for it were scrounged from reserve stocks and the training fleet. The route was transferred to Holloway upon Chalk Farm's closure in July 1993, and converted to O.P.O. at the end of March 1998.

Route 94 was introduced in September 1990 replacing the western section of route 88 between Acton Green and Marble Arch, and continuing to Trafalgar Square. In May 1992, RM1138 (S) heads along Regent Street. The 94 was RML-operated, but a number of RMs were kept at Shepherd's Bush Garage as spares for RMLs, especially when these were being refurbished between 1992 and 1994. The route converted to O.P.O. in January 2004.

Later in its career, route 10 was extended from Kings Cross to Tufnell Park along York Way, somewhat ironically replacing BL-operated route C11 on that section. On 3rd July 1993, RM2136 (HT) arrives at the latter terminus, which was actually Holloway Garage. By now, a number of RMs were there, and used indiscriminately with RMLs on the route until it was replaced at this end by the new 390 at the end of January 2003.

As a prelude to the privatisation of London Buses, a number of long-established central London routes were altered in July 1992. One was route 8, which was diverted at Bond Street to follow the former 25 routeing to Victoria. To replace it at its western end, a new route 98 was introduced running from Willesden Garage to Bloomsbury, using RMLs. A number of RMs were kept at Willesden to cover for RML refurbishment. One of them, a rather unkempt-looking RM1585 (AC), crosses Oxford Circus in August 1993. It has an RML nearside wing. The 98 converted to O.P.O. in March 2004.

Another 'new' route introduced in July 1992 was the 23, replacing the western section of route 15 between Ladbroke Grove and Paddington, paralleling it as far as Mansion House, and then continuing to Liverpool Street - its latter section also replacing route 9 east of Aldwych. However, the 23 was not really new at all, having run from Ladbroke Grove to Mansion House along the same route between 1981 and 1985 in conjunction with the 15. In January 1994, RM659 (X), another covering for RML refurbishments, overtakes RML2291 on the same route at Charing Cross. Of note are these two Routemasters' odd wings - the RM's nearside one is an RML one, whilst the RML has an RM nearside wing! Route 23 converted to O.P.O. at the end of October 2003, and has been withdrawn east of Aldwych as this book is being finalised.

The last new Routemaster-operated route of all was the 390, which was introduced on 1st February 2003 to replace route 10 between Archway (by then its northern terminus) and Kings Cross, then continuing to Marble Arch. On its first day, a freshly repainted RM646 (HT) crosses Oxford Circus as daylight fades. By now, this was one of the last RMs still in service with their original non-opening front upper-deck windows. It also bears Metroline's new 'blue skirt' livery. Route 390 converted to O.P.O. at the beginning of September 2004.

RETURN OF THE RM - 2

After route 29's conversion to O.P.O. in November 1988, most remaining Routemaster-operated services would retain them into the present century, although the 28 and 31 on the edge of the central London lost them in the spring of 1989 and routes 2, 3 and 88 also did in the early 1990s. Some RML-operated routes had increases in frequency, meaning that spare RMs had to be drafted in to make up the numbers. This happened with route 38, on which RM1185 (T) has been repainted in London Transport livery, complete with underlined gold fleetname, when heading west along Lea Bridge Road on 23rd February 1990 although the effect is spoilt by the non-standard numerals on its registration plate. This was the last day that the 38 ran east of Clapton Pond, yet it retained its extra RMs, which were transferred next day along with its main RML allocation from Leyton to Clapton Garage.

In the same area, route 73 also had a frequency increase during 1990, entailing the allocation of extra RMs to supplement its RMLs at Tottenham Garage. In September that year, RM1204 (AR) escorts RM995 (CT) past Islington Green; the latter being another of the 38's extras. The two routes ran parallel along Essex Road, parting company at Islington, Angel, then meeting again at Hyde Park Corner for the final run to Victoria. They converted to bendibus in 2004 (73) and 2005 (38), but today are operated by the so-called 'New Routemasters', but for how much longer?

In the last few weeks of route 13's operation from Finchley Garage, several RMs replaced its RML allocation to allow them to be released for refurbishment (or to replace RMLs elsewhere for the same purpose, if they had already been done), prior to the garage's loss of the route on tender to BTS of Borehamwood, and its closure. On the 13's last day of operation from Finchley, and north of Golders Green, re-registsred RM487 (FY) passes Daniels' Bagel Bakery in Temple Fortune on its way to Aldwych on 3rd December 1993.

Some RMs were also sent to other RML garages to cover for the latter when they were being refurbished. An example is RM342 (AC), which has also been repainted and re-registered, and nears its Red Lion Square terminus when heading along Bloomsbury Way on the new 98 route in September 1994. This route converted to O.P.O. in March 2004.

After a scare that it might be converted to single-deck O.P.O., which perhaps I helped avert by 'leaking' the plans to the local press, route 38 received another increase in frequency in 1997. A number of RMs were scrounged from elsewhere in the Cowie Group fleets (predecessor to Arriva London) and refurbished to provide the extra buses. Just after this happened, RM311 (CT) pauses outside its garage, Clapton, in August 1997. The route-branding shown here was applied also to some of the 38's existing RMLs, but not to all of them. Today, this part of Mare Street, colloquially known as the Narroway, is completely pedestrianised, and buses have to traverse the long one-way system taking them almost to Hackney Downs Station.

Two RMs 2033 and 2078 were also refurbished for London United, for whom they acted as spares to cover RMLs working from Shepherd's Bush Garage on routes 9 and 94. However, on 28th June 1998, they are to be found working special services 339 and 718 for the annual North Weald Bus Rally, of which I was one of the organisers.

By 6th August 1999, when RM980 (U) passes the Canning Town, Hermit Road terminus, London's buses had been privatised, and Stagecoach East London operated route 15. To provide extra buses to its RML operation, they brought back three of the RMs they had bought in the mid-1980s to operate in Scotland. This RM is one of them, which explains its Scottish registration.

The most drastic return of RMs of all was that of almost fifty of them, which were bought back by Transport for London, starting soon after its inception in 2000, and refurbished to bolster the existing fleet of surviving RMs and RMLs which, at the time, were likely to be kept going for at least another ten years. At first there were suggestions that at least one route might revert from O.P.O. to RM operation, but in the event, the vehicles were merely used to increase services on existing Routemaster-operated routes. The first entered service on route 13 in the summer of 2001, displacing its RMLs which were reallocated elsewhere. On 1st September 2001, RM45 (BT) loads up at Golders Green War Memorial on its first day back in service. As with many of the RMs reacquired, this one been sold for service in Scotland in the mid-1980s, though had not worked at London's service for some years before that, having been a radio trainer. In common with most of the RMs involved, it was refurbished by Marshalls of Cambridge and fitted with hopper windows. Quite why these were needed at the front upper-deck is a puzzle, since the RM had an early body with non-opening front windows anyway! RM45 had in the meantime been acquired from Strathtay Scottish by Reading MainLine before returning to London, where it was finally withdrawn in October 2005, when route 13 went O.P.O. after almost 43 years of Routemaster operation!

Further refurbished RMs, which were actually owned by TfL, appeared in the spring of 2002. RM875 (NX) was one of a handful sent to New Cross for route 36, on which it passes Marble Arch on a short working to Harrow Road, Prince of Wales on 23rd March 2002. It too had worked in Scotland, but for Kelvin Scottish in Glasgow rather than for Strathtay Scottish as RM45 had. When route 36 converted to O.P.O. in January 2005, it was passed on to Arriva, being used on route 19 and then 159 until the very end.

Also at Marble Arch on the same day is RM871 (X), one of a handful of these vehicles sent to Westbourne Park Garage to supplement RMLs on routes 7, on which it is turning short at North Kensington, Barlby Road, and 23. This one had worked for East Yorkshire in Hull in the late 1980s and early 1990s. Upon the 7's O.P.O. conversion in July 2004, it also went to Arriva's 19 and then 159, but was commandeered for use on the 15's 'heritage' service which it still works at the time of writing.

An oddity to appear at the same time was RM848 (S), sent to Shepherd's Bush Garage for routes 9 and 94. It was different in that it had the latest type of 'green' Euro engine, and also was in all-red livery, as clearly seen here passing Marble Arch on route 94, also on 23rd March 2002. This RM was also of note in that it carried the body (B847) that was on RM931 when that was out of action between 1973 and 1981. Eventually overhauled with a Leyland engine, it was sold to Blackpool Transport in the mid-1980s and later worked for Reading MainLine, another source of 'returnee' RMs for TfL. RM848 also passed to Arriva when Routemaster operation at Shepherds Bush ceased (on route 9 at the beginning of September 2004), ending its London days on route 38.

Despite the impending doom of the RMs, Arriva continued to refurbish those at Brixton Garage working routes 137 and 159. On 27th May 2002, RM997 (BN) had just been done when passing Hyde Park Corner on the 137. In addition to a fresh coat of paint, it has also gained new internal fittings, including fluorescent lighting, visible on its upper deck. This was one of the RMs that had borne the special 159 red and cream livery in the mid-1990s. Route 137 converted to O.P.O. in July 2004.

In the summer of 2002, route 38 received yet another service increase, necessitating nine extra buses! All of these were Marshall-refurbished returnees, and on 28th June 2002, a gleaming RM909 (CT) runs out of Clapton Garage for the evening rush hour. This, however, was to be the RMs' swansong. The 'disability lobby' had persuaded TfL to get rid of Routemasters after all, and the first of the surviving routes with them, the 10, would convert to O.P.O. in February 2003. The 38, which I have known since early childhood and also conducted in 1974/75, was the last route to operate RMs in north and north-east London, losing them at the end of October 2005, replaced by bendibuses of all things!

Because Marshall of Cambridge had gone out of business, the last handful of refurbished RMs were done by Arriva at their Ponders End Garage, and retained their existing windows. All went initially to Battersea for route 19, on which RM1292 (B) passes Tottenham Court Road Station on 20th September 2003. This was one of a few RMs that had been bought by TfL from preservationists. When the 19 converted to O.P.O., appropriately on April Fools Day 2005, it moved to route 159, where it stayed until the end.

Many of the TfL-owned refurbished RMs moved to their final home, route 159, as the routes they worked converted to O.P.O. in the last year of normal RM operation. On 16th July 2005, RM713 (BN), which had actually been re-imported from Italy where it had been used as a burger bar, heads through Kennington Triangle on 16th July 2005, having initially seen a couple of years' use on route 19 after refurbishment.

Perhaps as a sop to those outraged at the loss of London's RMs, two so-called 'heritage' services working over parts of previously RM- or RML-operated were introduced using a few of TfL's refurbished vehicles just before the last 'normal' RMs ran. One was a section of route 9 from Aldwych to Royal Albert Hall, where RM1280 (X) arrives on their first day, 14th November 2005. This RM had been bought from a preservationist, having previously worked routes 36, 19 and 159 after its return to London service.

The other 'heritage' RM service was a section of route 15 between Trafalgar Square and Tower Hill, from which RM1968 (U) sets off in the capable hands of my old friend Steve Few, also on the first day. At the time of writing, this service still - just about - operates, but that on the 9 was discontinued in July 2014.

LAST RITES

Long before the last RM ran at London's service, examples of the class operated special journeys for last days of various routes. Thus on 3rd September 1982, last day of route 94, RM2094 (TL) is specially dressed up to mark the occasion when departing from Lewisham Bus Station. A black waistband and wreath on its radiator grille are of note. The route had only fully converted from RT to RM just over four years previously, eliminating the last RTs in south London at the end of August 1978. However, initially route 94 was replaced by new RM-operated routes, the 208 and 261 but both converted to O.P.O. within the next two years.

Southern orbital route 37 had been one of the first to receive RMs in replacement for RT, in December 1962. On its last day of crew operation, 20th June 1986, my old friend Keith Molloy has donned a 1960s summer uniform, complete with white cap, when driving RM2013 (NX) on what was by then usually an RML-operated route. The bus is about to pass East Dulwich Station. Keith also drove the last RM home to New Cross Garage on route 53 in January 1988.

Right: RMs were sometimes fielded on last days of O.P.O. workings, too. A case in point was route 35. This had also converted to O.P.O. in June 1986, but when its journeys to Homerton Hospital were withdrawn as part of route changes in the area, RM14 (Q), the Camberwell Garage showbus, worked there specially on its last day, 23rd February 1990. It arrives at the hospital, driven by Pete Simmonds, another old friend of mine, and proceedings were soured somewhat by a security guard there trying to stop the dozens of enthusiasts taking photographs on 'his' territory! Although this was ridiculous or even inane, perhaps a drunken enthusiast aboard the bus who called the guard a few names that are unrepeatable in print did not help matters!

Below: It would be tedious to fill the pages of this book with pictures of the many RMs that worked specially on the last days of the final Routemaster-operated routes; besides my book 'Farewell Performance', now long out of print, did this adequately at the time. This view of RM5 (AR) is taken on the last day of crew operation on route 73, 3rd September 2004, heading up Park Lane and although this RM featured on 'last days' before and after the event, it was actually based at Tottenham, thus the 73 was its normal route. Of note is the large 'RM50' logo at the front between decks, marking the 50th anniversary of the appearance of RM1. Several of the surviving RMs and RMLs carried this at the time, but of course there was nothing really to celebrate as by then they were rapidly being withdrawn!

Although officially the last Routemaster at London's service on a normal route (the 159, on 9th December 2005) was RM2217, numerically the last 64-seat RM built, in actual fact RM54 (BN) was the last one home to its garage, because traffic congestion caused not least by the crowds attending the 'funeral' meant its journey to Streatham, and return to Brixton Garage, was considerably delayed. This view shows it climbing Brixton Hill on its final southbound journey. As may be observed, it is packed and also many of the crowds around it are there to mark the occasion. Also it is emblazoned with posters advertising the recently-introduced 'heritage' services using RMs on parts of route 9 and 15. RM54 is also of note in that it carries early body B31, so was over 46 years old at the time. It had been sold for use in Scotland in the mid-1980s, which explains its Scottish re-registration, and then bought back by TfL, having been one of the last to re-enter service in London, only in the spring of 2003. It was one of a handful of these returnees that were refurbished by Arriva at Ponders End Garage, and the only one to retain non-opening upper-deck front windows without the 'hopper' fixtures added.

END OF THE ROAD

Left: Barring a handful of fire and accident victims, no standard RMs were withdrawn until the infamous 'Law Lords' route cuts and O.P.O. conversions of 4th September 1982, brought about by the Tory-controlled London Borough of Bromley challenging the Labour-controlled Greater London Council's cheap fares policies, and being adjudged correct in the High Court. Around 200 RMs were withdrawn as a result, mostly those with Leyland engines and obsolete Sims electrical equipment. By pure chance, one of the first to go - in fact some time before the cuts actually took place - was RM496, which (numerically anyway!) I am pictured with down the 'Dilly when conducting it from Clapton Garage on route 38 on 8th May 1975.

Centre: Most of the RMs withdrawn upon the 'Law Lords' cuts were stored, still in running order, after withdrawal in a dealer's yard just outside the London Transport area in South-West Essex. On 16th September 1982, several of them are lined up here, with RM1100, 1752, 1588, 511 and 1739 nearest the camera. Almost as many dead DMSs were stored there too!

Below: The fact that the withdrawn RMs were stored in full view of a main road at a time when RM-operated routes not very far away were suffering from cancellations due to the dreaded 'no bus available syndrome' led to adverse reactions in the press, therefore most were moved to be secreted out of sight at Aldenham Works where, unfortunately, they were broken up by an outside contractor. On 9th October 1982, RM1773 and three others are just part of a procession of them I stumbled upon just by chance on the North Circular Road at Colney Hatch, on what turned out to be their last journeys to Aldenham. Sadly, several had only been overhauled there a few months previously.

Not long afterwards, some of these first withdrawals had found their way to the scrapyard of W, North's of Sherburn-In-Elmet, Yorkshire. On 29th October 1982, most there were still intact, but RM1297 was one of two on which scrapping had commenced.

After something of a lull in scrapping during 1983, RMs began to be broken up in ever-increasing numbers the following year. On 20th January 1984, RM1688 is one of several awaiting its fate at C.F. Booth's Rotherham yard, alongside contemporary British Railways Mk1 carriages. On the left is one of the ill-fated MD class, dating only from 1976, also due to be broken up.

As RM withdrawals accelerated, other scrapyards in Yorkshire took them. This harrowing scene at Wigley's Carlton yard on 30th August 1984 not only shows defunct RMs 1828 and 1634, but also two of the RCLs on which so much cost and effort had been expended to renovate as red buses just four years previously.

The skeletal remains of RM551 and RM1789 are also at Wigley's premises that day, surrounded by aluminium panels stripped from them, which could presumably be recycled.

At what would be the last of three Chiswick Works 'gala' open-days, on 11th August 1985, withdrawn RM1816 makes a sad sight when being used to demonstrate how buses are raised if they overturn as a result of accidents. Although tipped over several times during the two-day event, the RM suffered only superficial damage, most unlike DMSs whose flimsy bodywork was distorted at only the first drop at previous demonstrations!

On a dismal 5th January 1986, rows of withdrawn RMs (and a few RCLs) are lined up in the yard of the former A.E.C. Works at Southall, where most RMs' mechanical parts had been manufactured and which the Thatcher regime had closed down a few years previously. However, not all of these went for scrap. Following deregulation of bus services in Scotland the previous October, many RMs had been snapped up for further use to compete with established O.P.O. services there, a trend that spread to England when services there too were deregulated in October 1986. Some of these RMs, and also the surviving RCLs, were also refurbished for the Original London Sightseeing Tour, as previously shown in this volume.

By the end of 1989, the rear yard of Fulwell Garage was used as a storage point for withdrawn vehicles, which included a number of RMs being reconditioned for sale for re-use. However, disaster struck during the Christmas/New Year period when vandals broke in and used the RMs as 'dodgems'! One of the victims was RM1745, smashed both back and front and with most windows broken. Therefore, several of them were damaged beyond repair, though their reconditioned running units were retrieved for use on other vehicles.

GARAGE CODES

The following garage codes are shown in brackets after the numbers of
RMs illustrated in this book:

A - Sutton
AC - Willesden
AD - Palmers Green
AE - Hendon
AF - Putney, Chelverton Road
AG - Ash Grove (Cambridge Heath)
AK - Streatham
AL - Merton
AM - Plumstead
AP - Seven Kings
AR - Tottenham
AV - Hounslow
AW - Abbey Wood
B - Battersea
BK - Barking
BN - Brixton
BT - BTS, Borehamwood/Edgware
BW - Bow
CF - Chalk Farm
CT - Clapton
D - Dalston
E - Enfield (Ponders End)
ED - Elmers End
EM - Edmonton
FW - Fulwell
FY - Finchley
GM - Victoria, Gillingham Street
H - Hackney
HD - Harrow Weald
HL - Hanwell
HT - Highgate (renamed Holloway, 4/9/71)
HW - Southall
J - Holloway (until 3/9/71)
K - Kingston
KC - Kings Cross (subsidiary of HT)
M - Mortlake
MH - Muswell Hill

N - Norwood
NB - Norbiton
NS - North Street, Romford
NX - New Cross
ON - Alperton
PB - Potters Bar
PM - Peckham
PR - Poplar
Q - Camberwell
R - Riverside (Hammersmith)
RD - Hornchurch
RL - Rye Lane, Peckham
S - Shepherd's Bush
SE - Stonebridge Park
SF - Stamford Hill
SP - Sidcup
SW - Stockwell
T - Leyton
TB - Bromley
TC - South Croydon
TH - Thornton Heath
TL - Catford
U - Upton Park
UX - Uxbridge
V - Turnham Green (until 9/5/80)
V - Stamford Brook (from 10/5/80)
W - Cricklewood
WD - Wandsworth
WH - West Ham
WL - Walworth
WN - Wood Green
WW - Walthamstow
X - Middle Row, North Kensington (until 14/8/81)
X - Westbourne Park (from 15/8/81)

Main Cover Photo: On 16th October 1976, RM402 (WW) passes Southgate Town Hall on its way from Enfield Town to Walthamstow. This trolleybus replacement route had been re-routed from Tottenham to Enfield in replacement of the 275 upon the first stage of the Reshaping Plan on 7th September 1968, also replacing the northern end of route 269, and converted to DMS O.P.O. in March 1977.

Bottom Left Cover Photo: Tram replacement route 109 took several months to convert from RT to RM operation in 1976, only to lose them in favour of crew DMs two years later. Shortly before that happened, RM1239 (TH) approaches the junction of Brixton Hill and Upper Tulse Hill on 17th August 1978. RMs returned to the route in 1981/82, but it converted to O.P.O. in February 1987.

Bottom Right Cover Photo: Early-bodied RM35 (AD) loads up at the Enfield Town, Palace Gardens terminus of route 29 on 8th July 1978. Converted to RM operation on 7th September 1968, the busy 29 was diverted and extended to Enfield Town to replace the northern section of route 123 in March 1977. It converted to Metrobus O.P.O. in November 1988, being the last RM-operated route in outer north London.

Frontispiece Photo: St, Mary-le-Strand church forms the backdrop to this view of RM826 (AC) at Aldwych in April 1923. This church dates from the 1720s, although there had been earlier buildings on the site. It was badly damaged during the 1940 blitz. Route 6 had been withdrawn east of Aldwych in July 1992, and the RM is standing in for RMLs being refurbished at this time. The route converted to O.P.O. in March 2004.

Back Cover Photo: Illustrating the standard rear-end arrangement of all RMs and RMLs, RM715 (AD) has just run in to Palmers Green Garage on 4th November 1988, the last day of RM operation on my local route 29 and also at my local garage. Of note is the offside advertisement arrangement, and the London Buses 'bullseye' logo, both of which were recent innovations. This was also RM715's last day in service. It was subsequently exported to Japan!